The **HUT(**

GCSE
Revision
Quiz Book

Copyright © Helicon Publishing 2001

Helicon Publishing Ltd
42 Hythe Bridge Street
Oxford OX1 2EP
United Kingdom
E-mail: admin@helicon.co.uk
Web site: http://www.helicon.co.uk

First published 2001

ISBN: 1-85986-359-0

British Library Cataloguing in Publication Data
A catalogue record for this book is available from the British Library.

Typeset by Florence Production Ltd
Stoodleigh, Devon
Printed and bound in Great Britain by
Cox & Wyman Ltd, Reading, Berkshire

Acknowledgements

Project Management
Sparrowhawk and Heald Ltd

Contributors
Glennis Atkinson, specialist and examiner in Religious Education
Judy Bell, teacher of Music
Stephen Drew, teacher of History
Gordon Erhorn, teacher of Design
Richard Gill, teacher of Science
Wilf Hodgson, Mathematics specialist and editor
Keith Lawn, teacher of Biology
Graham Loasby, ICT coordinator
Gina Patterson, ICT tutor
Joyce Shorrock, teacher of Chemistry
Jacqueline Thornborrow, teacher of Geography
Pete Townsend, freelance writer and lecturer in Business Studies
Sue Williams, teacher of English, Drama, and PSHE

Editorial Director
Hilary McGlynn

Deputy Editorial Director
Roger Tritton

Project Editor
Clare Collinson

Technical Project Editor
Rachel Margolis

Editors
Andrew Bacon
Denise Dresner
Joan Lait
Nicky Matthews
Catherine Thompson
Lisa Trueman

Content Development Manager
Claire Lishman

Content Fulfilment Manager
Tracey Auden

Production Manager
John Normansell

Production Controller
Stacey Penny

Design Manager
Lenn Darroux

Page Design
Paul Saunders

Contents

Preface

Revision requires a lot of planning, organization, and learning, and it is important to make the most of your time. GCSE students will find that these fun and informative quick-fire questions provide an antidote to the rigours of other forms of revision!

Written and checked by classroom teachers, the questions and answers are designed to complement your classroom learning and home study work. By testing yourself you will be able to confirm and consolidate what you know and make progress in areas of weakness.

Organized into 12 subject areas, *The Hutchinson GCSE Revision Quiz Book* covers the core National Curriculum subjects as well as optional GCSE subjects such as Business Studies. Each subject has been divided up into subsections, based on the key areas of the National Curriculum programmes of study. So you can either work your way steadily through all of the questions in a subject, or go straight to the topic you wish to revise. If you are unsure which topics you need to cover, you should ask your teacher.

In the Mathematics section you will find questions at various levels of difficulty, some appropriate to the foundation programme of study, some intermediate, and some appropriate to the higher programme of study. The Biology, Chemistry, and Physics sections include questions appropriate for students studying the Single Science or Double Science programmes, as well as those who are following separate GCSE courses in all three sciences.

Each question is numbered consecutively within its section. The correct answers to the questions can be found by referring to the appropriate subject in the answers section at the back of the book, pages 180–183.

Good luck with your revision and have fun while the essentials sink in!

English
Questions

1 Which of the following is a theme in Shakespeare's *Romeo and Juliet*?

- a. Mercutio's speech on 'Queen Mab'
- b. Iambic pentameter
- c. Intelligence
- d. Love

2 Which of the following is **not** a play by Shakespeare?

- a. *As You Like It*
- b. *Othello*
- c. *Pygmalion*
- d. *King Lear*

3 What is the 'plot' in a story or novel?

- a. Where the story is set
- b. The opening of the story
- c. The storyline
- d. The twist in the story

4 What can a 'theme' be defined as?

- a. The title of a poem
- b. A subject that a writer wishes to bring to the reader's attention
- c. The kind of language a writer uses
- d. The hidden message in a piece of writing

5 What is a sub-plot?

- a. The main plot of the story
- b. A setting that is of little importance to the main plot
- c. The main setting
- d. A storyline that is additional to the main plot

6 How would you refer to a person in a novel?

- a. An actor
- b. A cast
- c. A woman or man
- d. A character

Poetry

7 When is a poem more likely to appear orderly and controlled?

- a. When it uses a balanced number of verbs and nouns
- b. When it uses a fixed, steady metre
- c. When there is an even number of stanzas
- d. When the narrative is clear and simple

1

8 What is the rhythm of a poem?

☐ a. The stanza
☐ b. The metre
☐ c. Assonance
☐ d. The structure

9 What are the separate sections of a poem called?

☐ a. Chapters
☐ b. Segments
☐ c. Paragraphs
☐ d. Stanzas

10 If the metre in a poem is regular, what does this mean?

☐ a. There is no pattern of rhyme in the poem
☐ b. There is no particular pattern of rhythm in the poem
☐ c. There is a certain pattern of rhythm throughout the poem
☐ d. There is a pattern of rhyme in the poem

11 What name is given to two lines, one after the other, that have the same rhyme?

☐ a. A rhyming couplet
☐ b. Blank verse
☐ c. Double rhymed
☐ d. A simile

12 Which of these poems is a sonnet?

☐ a. 'Stealing' by Carol Anne Duffy
☐ b. 'Hurricane hits England' by Grace Nichols
☐ c. 'Cataract Operation' by Simon Armitage
☐ d. 'I Am Very Bothered' by Simon Armitage

13 What is the general term for poetry that rhymes?

☐ a. Verse
☐ b. Limerick
☐ c. Song
☐ d. Ballad

14 Which of these does not relate to imagery?

☐ a. Personification
☐ b. Assonance
☐ c. Metaphor
☐ d. Simile

15 Carol Anne Duffy uses the image of an onion in her poem 'Valentine'. Which of the following explains why?

☐ a. To make the poem humorous
☐ b. To provide what she considers to be a more truthful view of love
☐ c. To show how terrible a relationship the lovers have
☐ d. To add to the other tastes in the poem

16 Which poet wrote 'I Wanna Be Yours'?

☐ a. John Agard
☐ b. John Cooper Clarke
☐ c. Stevie Smith
☐ d. Fleur Adcock

17 Which of these poems by Simon Armitage contains some elements of a love poem?

☐ a. 'Poem'
☐ b. 'About his Person'
☐ c. 'I Am Very Bothered'
☐ d. 'Cataract Operation'

18 Which of these poems contains a character whose mother has died?

- [ ] a. 'Rapunzstiltskin' by Liz Lochead
- [ ] b. 'Half Caste' by John Agard
- [ ] c. 'I Am Very Bothered' by Simon Armitage
- [ ] d. 'For Heidi with Blue Hair' by Fleur Adcock

19 Which of these events does not happen in a poem by Carol Anne Duffy?

- [ ] a. A soldier dreaming of going home
- [ ] b. A young child asking about how they were born
- [ ] c. A man developing photographs
- [ ] d. The theft of a snowman

20 Which of these poems by Carol Anne Duffy is not written in the first person?

- [ ] a. 'Before You Were Mine'
- [ ] b. 'Valentine'
- [ ] c. 'Stealing'
- [ ] d. 'War Photographer'

21 In which poem by Carol Anne Duffy does the narrator call themself 'a mucky ghost'?

- [ ] a. 'Valentine'
- [ ] b. 'Mrs. Tilscher's Class'
- [ ] c. 'Stealing'
- [ ] d. 'War Photographer'

22 Which of the following poems uses Gujerati as well as English?

- [ ] a. 'Hurricane hits England' by Grace Nichols
- [ ] b. 'Half Caste' by John Agard
- [ ] c. 'Presents from my Aunts in Pakistan' by Moniza Alvi
- [ ] d. 'Search for My Tongue' by Sujata Bhatt

23 Which of the following themes is not dealt with in John Agard's 'Half Caste'?

- [ ] a. Colour
- [ ] b. Identity
- [ ] c. Naming
- [ ] d. Fear

24 Which of the following poems was written before 1900?

- [ ] a. 'Song of the Worms' by Margaret Atwood
- [ ] b. 'To his Coy Mistress' by Andrew Marvell
- [ ] c. 'The World is a Beautiful Place' by Lawrence Ferlinghetti
- [ ] d. 'Before You Were Mine' by Carol Anne Duffy

25 What would you need to do if asked to compare two poems?

- [ ] a. Decide which poem is the best
- [ ] b. Write about one poem, then write about the other one
- [ ] c. Find ways in which the poems are similar
- [ ] d. Find criticisms of each poem

26 Which of these is a type of poem?

- [ ] a. Sonnet
- [ ] b. Hyperbole
- [ ] c. Kenning
- [ ] d. Prose

27 When answering an examination question on poems, which of these is not necessary?

- ☐ a. Telling the story of what happens in the poems
- ☐ b. Using quotations to support your points
- ☐ c. Checking your work carefully when you finish
- ☐ d. Checking to make sure that you are answering the question throughout your answer

28 When writing about the form of a poem, which of the following need you not look for?

- ☐ a. The length of the lines
- ☐ b. Whether the poem is divided into stanzas
- ☐ c. The way the words are set out on the page
- ☐ d. The imagery of the poem

29 When revising poetry in your anthology, which of these is least advisable?

- ☐ a. Thinking about common themes in a set of poems by the same writer
- ☐ b. Making sure you understand all the words in each poem, using a dictionary if you are unsure
- ☐ c. Reading the poems again and again as the main part of your revision
- ☐ d. Looking at what the words and images suggest

30 Which of the following poets wrote a parody of the language used by BBC newsreaders?

- ☐ a. John Agard
- ☐ b. Ted Hughes
- ☐ c. Sujata Bhatt
- ☐ d. Tom Leonard

31 Which of the following is **not** a form of poetry?

- ☐ a. Anticlimax
- ☐ b. Ballad
- ☐ c. Kenning
- ☐ d. Sonnet

Language, grammar, and punctuation

32 What is a noun?

- ☐ a. A person, place, or object
- ☐ b. A piece of punctuation
- ☐ c. A type of verb
- ☐ d. A describing word

33 Which of these is a noun?

- ☐ a. Quickly
- ☐ b. Walked
- ☐ c. Shirt
- ☐ d. The

34 Which of these describes a verb?

- ☐ a. A person, place, or object
- ☐ b. A word that describes a noun
- ☐ c. An action or doing word
- ☐ d. A describing word

35 Which of the following cannot be used as an adjective?

- ☐ a. Speedy
- ☐ b. Runny
- ☐ c. Fiercely
- ☐ d. Tall

36 Which of these words is not an adverb?

- ☐ a. Quickly
- ☐ b. Excitedly
- ☐ c. Wisely
- ☐ d. Tiny

37 What is an abstract noun?

- ☐ a. A noun that names a feeling or state
- ☐ b. A doing word
- ☐ c. A living thing
- ☐ d. A noun that names something concrete

38 To which word type do the words 'hope' and 'misery' belong?

- ☐ a. Pronouns
- ☐ b. Verbs
- ☐ c. Abstract nouns
- ☐ d. Adverbs

39 Which of the following words cannot be used as a noun?

- ☐ a. Hope
- ☐ b. Sunny
- ☐ c. Head
- ☐ d. Walk

40 Which of the following word types can add movement and action to a piece of writing?

- ☐ a. Pronouns
- ☐ b. Adverbs
- ☐ c. Verbs
- ☐ d. Nouns

41 Which of the following is an adjective?

- ☐ a. Thoughtless
- ☐ b. Slowly
- ☐ c. Cat
- ☐ d. Skip

42 Which of the following is a noun?

- ☐ a. Rolled
- ☐ b. Hopefully
- ☐ c. Wheel
- ☐ d. Climbing

43 Which of the following is a pronoun?

- ☐ a. Grass
- ☐ b. She
- ☐ c. To
- ☐ d. For

44 Which of the following is **not** a preposition?

- ☐ a. By
- ☐ b. On
- ☐ c. After
- ☐ d. And

45 Which of the following is an adverb?

- ☐ a. Messily
- ☐ b. Phone
- ☐ c. Tree
- ☐ d. Small

46 Which of the following is a verb?

- ☐ a. Car
- ☐ b. Think
- ☐ c. Green
- ☐ d. Little

47 To what parts of speech do 'practice' and 'practise' belong?

- ☐ a. Adverb, noun
- ☐ b. Noun, adverb
- ☐ c. Noun, verb
- ☐ d. Verb, noun

48 To what parts of speech do 'advice' and 'advise' belong?

- ☐ a. Adverb, noun
- ☐ b. Verb, noun
- ☐ c. Noun, verb
- ☐ d. Noun, adverb

49 What is a simile?

- ☐ a. The repetition of similar vowel sounds
- ☐ b. A word with an opposite meaning to another
- ☐ c. A word with a similar meaning to another
- ☐ d. A comparison between two things using 'as' or 'like'

50 Which of the following is a simile?

- ☐ a. She was fast and clumsy like a bull in a china shop
- ☐ b. The cold ate away at me
- ☐ c. As I got into the car, it began to rain heavily
- ☐ d. There were two girls, each smiling in the same way

51 Which of these is a metaphor?

- ☐ a. Beautiful, buzzing bees made honey
- ☐ b. I could smell roses as I walked down the flowery drive
- ☐ c. The birds pecked at their seeds like greedy children
- ☐ d. The sun was a golden coin shining in the sky

52 Why might a writer use a metaphor?

- ☐ a. To create suspense by slowing down the pace of the writing
- ☐ b. To enable the reader to get a picture of something more vividly
- ☐ c. To provide a clear summary of an idea
- ☐ d. To make the writing very formal

53 Which of the following words contains not more than three consonants?

- ☐ a. Part
- ☐ b. Hopeless
- ☐ c. Pretty
- ☐ d. Tangerine

54 Which of the following is written in direct speech?

- ☐ a. 'Don't forget your bag!', shouted Mira
- ☐ b. The castle looked huge, even from a distance
- ☐ c. She spoke slowly and clearly
- ☐ d. James explained how he had lost the dog

55 Which of the following is written in indirect speech?

- ☐ a. Amy whispered that she couldn't find her book
- ☐ b. What a lot of mess there was in the kitchen!
- ☐ c. The sun was setting when they arrived
- ☐ d. 'I'm sorry,' said Sam

56 Which of the following is written in the imperative?

- ☐ a. There's a wonderful lake near the forest
- ☐ b. There was a full moon yesterday
- ☐ c. Where are my keys?
- ☐ d. Put the keys back under the mat when you've finished

57 Which of the following is most likely to contain imperatives?

- ☐ a. A thesaurus
- ☐ b. A recipe
- ☐ c. A dictionary
- ☐ d. A metaphor

58 What is jargon?

- ☐ a. The effective use of language in a piece of writing
- ☐ b. The style of writing associated with media texts
- ☐ c. Special words and terms used by a particular group or profession
- ☐ d. The use of feelings in poetry

59 Which of the following is not a metaphor?

- ☐ a. The rain spattered the window with water
- ☐ b. It was raining cats and dogs
- ☐ c. The dog shot across the room to get his dinner
- ☐ d. The burning heat ate into her skin

60 Which of these words is an example of onomatopoeia?

- ☐ a. Conclusion
- ☐ b. Walk
- ☐ c. Hiss
- ☐ d. Very

61 Which of the following best describes the word 'slithering'?

- ☐ a. Emotive
- ☐ b. Onomatopoeic
- ☐ c. Alliterative
- ☐ d. Monosyllabic

62 Which of these sentences is an example of personification?

- ☐ a. The fox ran swiftly
- ☐ b. All the people in the crowd looked excited
- ☐ c. The moon opened her big bright eye
- ☐ d. He ran like the wind

63 What is a pun?

- ☐ a. A piece of punctuation
- ☐ b. A play on words
- ☐ c. The main character in a story or play
- ☐ d. An image comparing one thing with another

64 Which of these sentences contains a pun?

- ☐ a. He always whines when we drink wine
- ☐ b. The slithering snakes moved slowly
- ☐ c. Don't touch that chocolate!
- ☐ d. The sun was as golden as a coin

65 Which of these words means a use of slang language?

- ☐ a. Direct speech
- ☐ b. Colloquialism
- ☐ c. Intonation
- ☐ d. Deterioration

66 What is hyperbole?

☐ a. Internal rhyme
☐ b. Understatement
☐ c. The use of abstract nouns in a text
☐ d. Exaggeration

67 What is a synonym?

☐ a. A form of poetry
☐ b. A comparison that likens one thing with another using 'as' or 'like'
☐ c. A word that describes an action
☐ d. A word with a near or identical meaning to another

68 Which of the following is not a synonym for 'beautiful'?

☐ a. Gorgeous
☐ b. Creamy
☐ c. Lovely
☐ d. Attractive

69 What is a metaphor?

☐ a. A word which is very similar to another word
☐ b. A word which has a double meaning
☐ c. A word that describes a verb
☐ d. A special comparison where one thing is described as if it were something else

70 What is onomatopoeia?

☐ a. A word with the opposite meaning to another word
☐ b. When the sound of a word suits its meaning
☐ c. When two words have a similar sound
☐ d. A word with a similar meaning to another word

71 Which of the following is an example of alliteration?

☐ a. He jumped like a kangaroo
☐ b. I knew how blue he felt
☐ c. Wild and whirling words
☐ d. She grew stronger and stronger

72 Which of the following is an example of assonance?

☐ a. How would you feel if someone spoke to you like that?
☐ b. The baby was curled up like a kitten
☐ c. Easy to please
☐ d. A whole army could not have kept me away

73 Which of the following is a metaphor?

☐ a. A hundred thoughts came into my head at once
☐ b. A sharp pain in my stomach
☐ c. A glimmer of hope
☐ d. The soft slithering of snakes

74 Which of the following is an example of onomatopoeia?

☐ a. A little bit
☐ b. Don't do that!
☐ c. The rain fell and fell
☐ d. Cock-a-doodle-doo

75 Which of the following adjectives does not suit the mood of the other three?

☐ a. Dreary
☐ b. Smooth
☐ c. Dull
☐ d. Greyish

76 Which of the following verbs does not suit the mood of the other three?

☐ a. Jumped
☐ b. Skipped
☐ c. Ran
☐ d. Thought

77 What best describes dialogue?

☐ a. Description
☐ b. Speech
☐ c. Conversation
☐ d. Indirect speech

78 Which of the following is an example of exaggeration?

☐ a. Laura's hand hurt ever so much
☐ b. Lots of people had come to see Paul play golf
☐ c. Are you sure you put it back?
☐ d. I kicked the ball so far that it must have reached Australia

79 Which of the following adverbs does not suit the mood of the other three?

☐ a. Swiftly
☐ b. Calmly
☐ c. Gently
☐ d. Soothingly

80 Which of the following uses an apostrophe correctly?

☐ a. I wore Simons' socks
☐ b. I wore Simons sock's
☐ c. I wore Simons socks'
☐ d. I wore Simon's socks

81 Which of the following sentences is wrongly punctuated?

☐ a. Why is there never any milk in the fridge.
☐ b. I wish the post would come on time.
☐ c. There were apples, pears, and bananas.
☐ d. 'Don't look!' shouted Paul.

82 Which of the following sentences is wrongly punctuated?

☐ a. I didn't want to go swimming.
☐ b. There we were, just the two of us, in the middle of the pouring rain.
☐ c. 'Quick!' shouted Sally.
☐ d. I'm hungry, moaned Sinbad.

83 Which of the following uses an exclamation mark correctly?

☐ a. I write to complain about the poor quality of service I recently received from your staff!
☐ b. 'Where on earth are you going!' asked Dad.
☐ c. 'I don't believe it!!!' yelled the customer.
☐ d. 'Stop it!' I shouted.

84 How should you begin a new sentence?

☐ a. Move to a new line
☐ b. Use a capital letter
☐ c. Use a comma
☐ d. Use a full stop

85 Which of the following would be least likely to contain bullet points?

☐ a. A leaflet
☐ b. An article

☐ c. An advice sheet
☐ d. A piece of descriptive writing

86 Which of the following needs a question mark?

☐ a. Look how rainy it is today
☐ b. If it was sunny we could play football
☐ c. I couldn't go to the party
☐ d. What will you wear to the party

87 Which of these sentences is correctly punctuated?

☐ a. Susan brought a cake some lemonade, and some of Richards muffin's.
☐ b. Susan brought a cake, some lemonade, and some of Richards' muffins.
☐ c. Susan brought a cake, some lemonade, and some of Richard's muffins.
☐ d. Susan brought a cake, some lemonade, and some of Richards muffins.

88 Which piece of punctuation must always go at the end of a rhetorical question?

☐ a. A full stop
☐ b. An exclamation mark
☐ c. A question mark
☐ d. A comma

89 What is a general word for the rules combining words into phrases, clauses, sentences, and paragraphs?

☐ a. Sentencing
☐ b. Grammar
☐ c. Punctuation
☐ d. Paragraphing

Spelling and vocabulary

90 Which of the following books is the most useful for widening your vocabulary?

☐ a. An encyclopedia
☐ b. A dictionary
☐ c. A thesaurus
☐ d. A dictionary of quotations

91 Which of these spellings is correct?

☐ a. Alliterasion
☐ b. Allitteration
☐ c. Alliteration
☐ d. Aliteration

92 Which of these spellings is correct?

☐ a. Bilive
☐ b. Bilieve
☐ c. Belive
☐ d. Believe

93 Which of these spellings is correct?

☐ a. Simmile
☐ b. Simile
☐ c. Simele
☐ d. Similie

94 Which of these spellings is incorrect?

☐ a. Alliteration
☐ b. Image
☐ c. Metaphor
☐ d. Ryhme

95 Which of these spellings is correct?

☐ a. Caracter
☐ b. Character
☐ c. Carachter
☐ d. Characta

96 Which of these spellings is incorrect?

- [ ] a. Plaine
- [ ] b. Plan
- [ ] c. Plane
- [ ] d. Plain

97 Which of these spellings is correct?

- [ ] a. Colloqualism
- [ ] b. Colloquialism
- [ ] c. Colloquiallsm
- [ ] d. Coloquialism

98 Which of these spellings is correct?

- [ ] a. Onomatopoeia
- [ ] b. Onomatopoiea
- [ ] c. Onomatopoia
- [ ] d. Onomatopoea

99 Which of the following spells the poet's name correctly?

- [ ] a. Ted Hues
- [ ] b. Ted hughs
- [ ] c. Ted Hughes
- [ ] d. Ted hyues

100 Which of these sentences is correctly spelt and punctuated?

- [ ] a. I bought some cakes for fifty pence each.
- [ ] b. I brought some cake's for fifty pence each.
- [ ] c. I bought some cake's for fifty pence each.
- [ ] d. I brought some cakes for fifty pence each.

Writing purposes and forms

101 Which of the following helps to organize text for the reader?

- [ ] a. Using imagery
- [ ] b. Using exclamation marks
- [ ] c. Using paragraphs
- [ ] d. Using alliteration

102 How can you tell if text is written in the first person?

- [ ] a. The writer is objective
- [ ] b. The writer uses a formal style
- [ ] c. The writer addresses the audience as 'you' and him or herself as 'I'
- [ ] d. The writer uses bias

103 Which of the following would least suit a set of instructions?

- [ ] a. Using alliteration and assonance
- [ ] b. Making sure there is not too much information
- [ ] c. Using clear, precise language
- [ ] d. Using the imperative

104 What is the conclusion to an essay?

- [ ] a. The structure of the essay
- [ ] b. The main core of the essay
- [ ] c. An ending to the essay which sums up the findings
- [ ] d. The opening of the essay which introduces the topic

105 When you quote from a text, what should you do?

- [ ] a. Begin a new paragraph
- [ ] b. Miss a line before introducing the quote

☐ c. Use quotation marks
☐ d. Underline the quote

☐ c. There are museums in London
☐ d. The Queen lives in London

106 What is a narrator?

☐ a. The author of the text
☐ b. The storyline
☐ c. A character who tells the story
☐ d. The main character

107 Which of these statements is an opinion?

☐ a. The table is made from oak
☐ b. The cinema shows films at the weekend
☐ c. That shirt is made from excellent fabric
☐ d. It is possible to be allergic to animal hair

108 Why is suspense effective?

☐ a. It provides the reader with immediate satisfaction
☐ b. It involves the reader fully in a character's feelings
☐ c. It allows the reader to feel strong feelings
☐ d. It keeps the reader interested in the text

109 Which of these techniques does not add detail to writing?

☐ a. Adding adjectives
☐ b. Summarizing
☐ c. Using all five senses in the writing
☐ d. Using imagery

110 Which of the following is an opinion?

☐ a. London is the capital of England
☐ b. London is a beautiful city

111 Which of these techniques is most likely to give the writer authority?

☐ a. Using bold print and underlining
☐ b. Clearly structuring the argument
☐ c. Using a wide range of emotive language
☐ d. Using specialist language and technical terms

112 Why is 'They jumped for sheer joy!' an example of emotive language?

☐ a. Because it is very biased
☐ b. Because the words 'joy' and 'jumped' both begin with the same letter
☐ c. Because it uses the words 'sheer joy' which are full of feeling
☐ d. Because it uses direct speech

113 If the writer wants the reader to feel relaxed and closely involved, what will he or she be most likely to do?

☐ a. Use subheadings
☐ b. Use a formal style
☐ c. Use indirect speech
☐ d. Use an informal style

114 Which of these does not help to create suspense?

☐ a. Telling the reader only some of the necessary information
☐ b. Using a cliffhanger at the end of a chapter
☐ c. Giving the reader all the available information about a character

d. Allowing the reader to know something important that the character does not know

115 Which word means the hidden message of a poem or piece of writing?

a. Highlight
b. Context
c. Indentation
d. Subtext

116 What is a rhetorical question?

a. A question requiring an answer
b. A trick question
c. A difficult question to answer
d. A question asked for effect, not requiring an answer

117 Why might you use a rhetorical question in a piece of persuasive writing?

a. To make the reader angry
b. To get an answer from the reader
c. To add suspense
d. To encourage the reader to consider what you are suggesting

118 What is empathy?

a. A close friendship between two people
b. The ability to identify with the feelings of others
c. The ability to communicate with another person
d. The feelings raised by a piece of writing

119 What is an anticlimax?

a. The use of contrast to draw the audience's attention to a detail
b. A buildup in the audience's expectations

c. When an outcome does not meet the audience's expectations
d. The high point the audience has been waiting for

120 Why are bullet points effective in an article?

a. They add to the description in the article
b. They create suspense
c. They provide a clear, definite list
d. They can be used instead of paragraphs

121 When commenting on how ideas are presented in a leaflet, which of the following would you not comment on?

a. Illustrations
b. The use of facts and opinions
c. The different uses of print
d. The layout of the leaflet

122 In a letter to a friend, where should the writer's address be placed?

a. Bottom right
b. Bottom left
c. Top left
d. Top right

123 Which of the following sentences would be the least suitable for a formal letter?

a. You've made a complete pig's ear out of that dump of a car park
b. I believe the school would benefit from a new playground
c. Please reply explaining how you intend to deal with this problem
d. It would make the town feel much safer if High Street was better lit

124 Which of the following is the story of somebody's life?

- ☐ a. Biography
- ☐ b. Litotes
- ☐ c. Report
- ☐ d. Diplomacy

125 Which of the following is a fiction text?

- ☐ a. A newspaper article
- ☐ b. A play script
- ☐ c. An autobiography
- ☐ d. A film review

126 What is unlikely to make for a good short story written in an examination?

- ☐ a. Planning the events in the story
- ☐ b. A very detailed plot
- ☐ c. A simple plot
- ☐ d. Using adjectives, similes, and other descriptive techniques

127 Which of these does not help to organize ideas?

- ☐ a. Onomatopoeia
- ☐ b. Subheadings
- ☐ c. Paragraphs
- ☐ d. Bullet points

128 Which of the following do you not need to do when answering an essay question?

- ☐ a. Copy out the essay question fully
- ☐ b. Proofread afterwards
- ☐ c. Plan before you start writing
- ☐ d. Give examples, to show the reader what you mean

129 Which of the following would not be used to create atmosphere in a text?

- ☐ a. Emotive language
- ☐ b. Description using all five senses
- ☐ c. Imagery
- ☐ d. Underlining and bold print

130 Which of the following means the place where events in a story happen?

- ☐ a. The setting
- ☐ b. The device
- ☐ c. The location
- ☐ d. The backdrop

131 Which of the following words is usually best avoided when writing a description?

- ☐ a. Nice
- ☐ b. Sunny
- ☐ c. Beautiful
- ☐ d. Clever

132 Which of the following would you use to sign off if you were writing a formal letter to someone whose name was unknown to you?

- ☐ a. With love
- ☐ b. Yours sincerely
- ☐ c. Your friend
- ☐ d. Yours faithfully

133 What are headlines designed to do?

- ☐ a. Catch the audience's attention
- ☐ b. Help the reader to understand the article or report
- ☐ c. Be clear, but uninteresting
- ☐ d. Provide a grammatically correct introduction to the article or report

134 Which of these is a non-fiction text?

- ☐ a. A ballad
- ☐ b. A newspaper article
- ☐ c. A novel
- ☐ d. A poem

135 What is a fact?

- ☐ a. A word that describes a noun
- ☐ b. Something that is true
- ☐ c. Something that is untrue
- ☐ d. A word that describes a verb

136 What does the first paragraph of a newspaper report often contain?

- ☐ a. An attempt to persuade the reader that the following points will be important
- ☐ b. The main points of the story
- ☐ c. A series of opinions about the event
- ☐ d. A brief interview with an individual

137 Which of the following is least likely to contain imagery?

- ☐ a. A formal letter
- ☐ b. A short story
- ☐ c. An advertisement
- ☐ d. A sports article

138 Which of these techniques is least likely to make an idea stand out?

- ☐ a. Placing it right at the end of a piece of writing
- ☐ b. Placing it in the centre paragraph of a piece of writing
- ☐ c. Repeating the idea, or words associated with it
- ☐ d. Exaggeration

139 Which of the following is bad advice for someone writing a descriptive piece?

- ☐ a. Use metaphors and similes to give the reader a clear picture
- ☐ b. Use paragraphs to organize your writing
- ☐ c. Avoid details so that the reader is not distracted from the storyline
- ☐ d. Try to appeal to all five senses

140 Which of the following forms of writing is an information text?

- ☐ a. A play script
- ☐ b. A ballad
- ☐ c. A leaflet
- ☐ d. A novel

141 Which of the following forms of writing would be unlikely to contain emotive language?

- ☐ a. A holiday brochure
- ☐ b. A sports article
- ☐ c. An advertisement
- ☐ d. A set of instructions

142 What is a parody?

- ☐ a. The repetition of sounds for effect
- ☐ b. A piece of imagery
- ☐ c. A humorous imitation of a style of writing or speech
- ☐ d. A contrast

143 Which of the following is not written in prose?

- ☐ a. A short story
- ☐ b. A poem
- ☐ c. A letter
- ☐ d. A diary

144 Which of the following does not show disagreement?

☐ a. On the other hand …
☐ b. Also …
☐ c. However …
☐ d. Although …

145 Which of the following effects cannot be brought about by repetition of a word or phrase?

☐ a. The creation of a certain mood in a passage
☐ b. A word or idea being made to seem more important
☐ c. An idea or word being made to stand out
☐ d. Variety of vocabulary

146 Which of the following is **not** a genre in writing?

☐ a. Poetry
☐ b. Play script
☐ c. Speech
☐ d. Collage

Standard English and language variation

147 Which of the following is not a dialect?

☐ a. West Indian
☐ b. Irish
☐ c. A Spanish accent
☐ d. Standard English

148 Which of these statements is not written in Standard English?

☐ a. There is also a great risk of flooding
☐ b. It is going to rain later today

☐ c. You is not listening to me!
☐ d. What is the time, please?

149 What is a dialect?

☐ a. A particular way of pronouncing words
☐ b. The way poets write
☐ c. A particular way of using words and grammar
☐ d. The way people speak on the news

150 Which of these poems is written in a Scottish dialect?

☐ a. A poem from 'Unrelated Incidents' by Tom Leonard
☐ b. 'An Old Woman' by Arun Kolatkar
☐ c. 'Ogun' by Edward Kamau Brathwaite
☐ d. 'The Thought Fox' by Ted Hughes

Mathematics
Questions

1 Solve the inequality $x^2 + 3 > 19$

- ☐ a. $-4 < x < 4$
- ☐ b. $x < -\sqrt[4]{2}$ or $x > \sqrt[4]{2}$
- ☐ c. $x < -4$ or $x > 4$
- ☐ d. $-\sqrt[4]{2} < x < \sqrt[4]{2}$

2 Simplify $3(2x - y) - 2(y - x)$

- ☐ a. $8x - 3y$
- ☐ b. $4x - 5y$
- ☐ c. $5x - 3y$
- ☐ d. $8x - 5y$

3 Fully factorize $6a + 9b - 3c$

- ☐ a. $3(2a + b) - 3c$
- ☐ b. $6a + 3(3b - c)$
- ☐ c. $3(2a + 3b - c)$
- ☐ d. $12abc$

4 Simplify $\dfrac{x}{2} + \dfrac{(x + 3)}{3}$

- ☐ a. $5x$
- ☐ b. $\dfrac{(2x + 3)}{6}$
- ☐ c. $\dfrac{(5x + 6)}{6}$
- ☐ d. $\dfrac{(2x + 3)}{5}$

5 Simplify $\dfrac{2}{x} + \dfrac{5}{(x + 1)}$

- ☐ a. $\dfrac{9}{(x + 1)}$
- ☐ b. $\dfrac{7}{(2x + 1)}$
- ☐ c. $\dfrac{(5x + 1)}{x}$
- ☐ d. $\dfrac{(7x + 2)}{x(x + 1)}$

6 Use trial and improvement to solve $x^3 + x = 27$ correct to two decimal places.

- ☐ a. 2.90
- ☐ b. 2.89
- ☐ c. 2.889
- ☐ d. 2.88

7 I think of a number. When I add 5 the answer is 12. What number did I think of?

- ☐ a. 17
- ☐ b. 5
- ☐ c. 12
- ☐ d. 7

8 I think of a number, double it, then add 3. The answer is 17. What number did I think of?

☐ a. 7
☐ b. 28
☐ c. 17
☐ d. 10

9 Solve $3(x + 7) = x + 31$

☐ a. $x = 5$
☐ b. $x = 9.5$
☐ c. $x = 11$
☐ d. $x = 12$

10 Solve this pair of simultaneous equations: $x + 2y = 6, 2x - y = 7$

☐ a. $x = 3.6, y = 1.7$
☐ b. $x = 2.7, y = 1.65$
☐ c. $x = 4, y = 1$
☐ d. $x = 1, y = 4$

11 A cinema has two prices for tickets, normal price for adults, and reduced rate for children and senior citizens. The Patel family pay £15.40 for two adults, one senior citizen, and two children. Their friends the Rossini family pay £13.70 for one adult and four children. What is the price of each type of ticket?

☐ a. £4.80 and £2.40
☐ b. £9.33 and £1.52
☐ c. £4.10 and £2.40
☐ d. £4.10 and £2.05

12 Make x the subject of $R = \dfrac{(x + 1)}{(x + 2)}$

☐ a. $x = \dfrac{(1 + 2R)}{(1 + R)}$

☐ b. $x = 1 - 2R + \dfrac{x}{R}$

☐ c. $x = \dfrac{(1 - 2R)}{(R - 1)}$

☐ d. $x = R(x + 2) - 1$

13 Use the formula $C = \dfrac{5}{9}(F - 32)$

to find the value of C when $F = 59$

☐ a. 15
☐ b. 77
☐ c. 48.6
☐ d. 0.02

14 Rearrange $s = \dfrac{1}{2}(u + v)t$

to make t the subject of the formula.

☐ a. $t = 2s - u - v$
☐ b. $t = \dfrac{2s}{(u + v)}$

☐ c. $t = \dfrac{s}{2(u + v)}$

☐ d. $t = \dfrac{(2s - ut)}{v}$

15 Find the value of $3a - 2b$ when $a = 5$ and $b = -2$

☐ a. 11
☐ b. 13
☐ c. 15
☐ d. 19

16 Rearrange $A = B + C$ to make B the subject of the formula.

☐ a. $B = \dfrac{C}{A}$

☐ b. $B = \dfrac{A}{C}$

c. $B = C - A$
d. $B = A - C$

17 Make x the subject of $y = 2 - \dfrac{1}{x}$

a. $x = 2 - \dfrac{1}{y}$

b. $x = \dfrac{1}{(2 - y)}$

c. $x = \dfrac{1}{2} - y$

d. $x = \dfrac{1}{(y - 2)}$

18 Make x the subject of
$\dfrac{1}{z} = \dfrac{1}{y} + \dfrac{1}{x}$

a. $x = \dfrac{yz}{(y - z)}$

b. $x = y - z$

c. $x = \dfrac{yz}{(z - y)}$

d. $x = z - y$

19 Solve $5 - 2x < 11$

a. $x < 3$
b. $x < -3$
c. $x > -3$
d. $x > 3$

20 Multiply out the brackets and simplify $(x + 3)(x - 2)$

a. $x^2 + x - 6$
b. $x^2 - 5x + 6$
c. $x^2 - 6$
d. $x^2 + 5x - 6$

21 Factorize $x^2 - 5x - 6$

a. $(x - 1)(x - 6)$
b. $(x + 1)(x - 6)$
c. $(x + 2)(x - 3)$
d. $(x - 2)(x + 3)$

22 Factorize $4x^2 - 4x - 15$

a. $(4x - 3)(x + 5)$
b. $(2x - 5)(2x + 3)$
c. $(4x + 5)(x - 3)$
d. $(2x - 3)(2x + 5)$

23 Factorize $x^2 - 36$

a. $(x - 3)(x + 12)$
b. $(x + 4)(x - 9)$
c. $(x - 4)(x + 9)$
d. $(x + 6)(x - 6)$

24 Factorize $4x^2 - 16y^2$

a. $(2x - 4y)(2x + 4y)$
b. Not possible
c. $(2x - 4y)^2$
d. $(2x)^2 - (4y)^2$

25 Solve $(x - 3)(x + 2) = 0$

a. $x = 6$ or $x = -6$
b. $x = -3$ or $x = 2$
c. $x = 3$ or $x = -2$
d. $x = 0$

26 Solve $x(2x + 1) = 0$

a. $x = -\sqrt{\dfrac{1}{2}}$

b. $x = \sqrt{\dfrac{1}{2}}$

c. $x = 0$ or $x = -\dfrac{1}{2}$

d. $x = 0$ or $x = \dfrac{1}{2}$

27 Solve $x^2 - 6x - 16 = 0$

☐ a. $x = 1$ or $x = -16$
☐ b. $x = 4$ or $x = -4$
☐ c. $x = 8$ or $x = -2$
☐ d. $x = -8$ or $x = 2$

28 Solve $7x^2 + 8x + 1 = 0$

☐ a. $x = \dfrac{1}{7}$ or $x = -1$

☐ b. $x = \dfrac{1}{7}$ or $x = 1$

☐ c. $x = -\dfrac{1}{7}$ or $x = -1$

☐ d. $x = -\dfrac{1}{7}$ or $x = 1$

29 Solve $3 + 5x = 2x^2$

☐ a. $x = 3$ or $x = -\dfrac{1}{2}$

☐ b. $x = -3$ or $x = -1$
☐ c. $x = 1$ or $x = 3$

☐ d. $x = -3$ or $x = \dfrac{1}{2}$

30 Solve $x^2 - 7x + 3 = 0$, giving answers to two decimal places.

☐ a. $x = -10.04$ or $x = -3.96$
☐ b. $x = -6.54$ or $x = -0.46$
☐ c. $x = 6.54$ or $x = 0.46$
☐ d. $x = 10.04$ or $x = 3.96$

31 What is the equation of the line of symmetry of the graph
$y = (x - 3)(x + 5)$?

☐ a. $x = -1$
☐ b. $x = 0$
☐ c. $y = 0$
☐ d. $x = 1$

32 The graph of $y = f(x)$ is translated three units parallel to the y axis. What is the equation of the new graph?

☐ a. $y = f(x) + 3$
☐ b. $y = f(x + 3)$
☐ c. $y = 3f(x)$
☐ d. $y = f(3x)$

33 What are the next two terms in the sequence 2, 3, 5, 9, 17, … ?

☐ a. $33, 65$
☐ b. $23, 29$
☐ c. $25, 27$
☐ d. $25, 33$

34 What is the nth term of the sequence 2, 5, 8, 11, 14, … ?

☐ a. $3n + 1$
☐ b. $n + 3$
☐ c. $3n - 1$
☐ d. $n - 3$

35 Find the nth term of the sequence 3, 13, 28, 49, …

☐ a. $3n^2 + 1$
☐ b. $6n^2 - 2$
☐ c. $n^2 - 3n$
☐ d. $n^2 + 3$

Number

36 A monkey is trying to climb a slippery tree to reach some fruit 30 m above the ground. The monkey takes one second to climb 3 m but in the next second it slides down 2 m. How many seconds will it take the monkey to reach the fruit?

☐ a. 60 seconds
☐ b. 55 seconds
☐ c. 57 seconds
☐ d. 59 seconds

37 What is the value of 0.6×3?

☐ a. 3.6
☐ b. 2.4
☐ c. 1.8
☐ d. 0.18

38 An athlete's best time for the 400 m is 48.67 seconds. In her next race she runs 400 m in 47.93 seconds. By how much did she beat her previous best time?

☐ a. 0.74 seconds
☐ b. 1.34 seconds
☐ c. 0.26 seconds
☐ d. 0.34 seconds

39 Convert $0.\dot{2}\dot{7}$ into a fraction in its simplest terms.

☐ a. $\frac{27}{100}$
☐ b. $\frac{3}{11}$
☐ c. $\frac{27}{99}$
☐ d. $\frac{3}{10}$

40 The mass of a gem is measured in carats. One carat is 0.2.g. What is the mass of a 2500 carat diamond?

☐ a. 5000 g
☐ b. 5 g
☐ c. 500 g
☐ d. 50 g

41 Which of these numbers is not a factor of 12?

☐ a. 5
☐ b. 6
☐ c. 1
☐ d. 3

42 What is the highest common factor of 414 and 630?

☐ a. 18
☐ b. 2
☐ c. 9
☐ d. 6

43 Which fraction is the same as 25%?

☐ a. $\frac{3}{4}$
☐ b. $\frac{1}{4}$
☐ c. $2\frac{1}{2}$
☐ d. $\frac{1}{2}$

44 Write the reciprocal of 7.5 as a fraction.

☐ a. $\frac{2}{15}$
☐ b. $\frac{75}{10}$
☐ c. $7\frac{1}{2}$
☐ d. $\frac{15}{2}$

45 What is the value of 2^3?

☐ a. 8
☐ b. 23
☐ c. 16
☐ d. 6

46 What is half of 2^{20}?

☐ a. 1^{20}
☐ b. 1^{10}
☐ c. 2^{19}
☐ d. 2^{10}

47 Express 0.000000476 in standard form.

- [ ] **a.** 47.6×10^{-6}
- [ ] **b.** 476×10^{-5}
- [ ] **c.** 4.76×10^{-7}
- [ ] **d.** 4.76×10^{7}

48 Convert 7.9×10^{5} into a decimal number.

- [ ] **a.** 3,950
- [ ] **b.** 7,900,000
- [ ] **c.** 790,000
- [ ] **d.** 0.000079

49 Find the value of $64^{\frac{2}{3}}$.

- [ ] **a.** 2
- [ ] **b.** 512
- [ ] **c.** 16
- [ ] **d.** $4^{2\frac{2}{3}}$

50 What is another way of writing $a^{\frac{1}{2}}$?

- [ ] **a.** $\sqrt{a}$
- [ ] **b.** $\dfrac{a}{2}$
- [ ] **c.** $\dfrac{1}{2}a$
- [ ] **d.** $a \div 2$

51 What do you need to add to 34 to make 100?

- [ ] **a.** 66
- [ ] **b.** 56
- [ ] **c.** 76
- [ ] **d.** 46

52 Which of these is not a rational number?

- [ ] **a.** 23%
- [ ] **b.** 1

- [ ] **c.** $\dfrac{13}{25}$
- [ ] **d.** $\sqrt{2}$

53 Alice works a 38 hour week and is paid £4.80 per hour. How much does she earn per week?

- [ ] **a.** £182.40
- [ ] **b.** £7.92
- [ ] **c.** £152
- [ ] **d.** £1,824

54 Which of these is not a multiple of 6?

- [ ] **a.** 62
- [ ] **b.** 72
- [ ] **c.** 54
- [ ] **d.** 42

55 In a desert the temperature falls from 24°C at midday to −8°C at midnight. How many degrees does the temperature fall?

- [ ] **a.** 20
- [ ] **b.** 28
- [ ] **c.** 16
- [ ] **d.** 32

56 A restaurant adds a 12% service charge to each customer's bill.
A customer is asked to pay £12.32 for a meal including the service charge. What was the cost of the meal before the service charge was added?

- [ ] **a.** £10.84
- [ ] **b.** £12.20
- [ ] **c.** £10.88
- [ ] **d.** £11.00

57 A savings account pays 6.4% interest per annum. How much interest will an investment of £125 earn in one year?

- ☐ a. £8.00
- ☐ b. 64p
- ☐ c. 80p
- ☐ d. £6.40

58 A household electricity bill is £93.60. VAT is added at a rate of 5%. How much will the householder have to pay altogether?

- ☐ a. £98.28
- ☐ b. £98.60
- ☐ c. £46.80
- ☐ d. £140.40

59 A television set costs £680. It can be bought under a hire purchase agreement requiring a 20% cash deposit then 12 monthly payments of £52. How much more will it be to buy the television on hire purchase?

- ☐ a. £56
- ☐ b. £136
- ☐ c. £36
- ☐ d. £80

60 A tennis club has 49 members. Last year the tennis club only had 35 members. By what percentage has the membership increased?

- ☐ a. 40%
- ☐ b. 14%
- ☐ c. 71%
- ☐ d. 29%

61 Convert 80% into a fraction expressed in its simplest terms.

- ☐ a. $\frac{4}{5}$
- ☐ b. $\frac{40}{50}$
- ☐ c. $\frac{80}{100}$
- ☐ d. $\frac{8}{10}$

62 A house which cost £95,000 three years ago has risen in value by 20%. How much is it valued at now?

- ☐ a. £76,000
- ☐ b. £114,000
- ☐ c. £95,200
- ☐ d. £115,000

63 At a football match 45% of the supporters buy a pie at half time. If 5,175 supporters buy a pie, how many supporters attended the game?

- ☐ a. 2,329
- ☐ b. 11,500
- ☐ c. 2,846
- ☐ d. 9,409

64 Which of the following has the largest value?

- ☐ a. 62%
- ☐ b. $\frac{5}{8}$
- ☐ c. 0.59
- ☐ d. $\frac{43}{72}$

65 A personal stereo is reduced by 25% in a sale and now costs £60. What was its price before the sale?

- ☐ a. £75
- ☐ b. £45
- ☐ c. £85
- ☐ d. £80

66 A shirt costing £35 is reduced by 20% in a sale. What is the sale price of the shirt?

- ☐ a. £20
- ☐ b. £15
- ☐ c. £25
- ☐ d. £28

67 What is the value of the digit '3' in the number 542.371?

- ☐ a. Three hundredths
- ☐ b. Three tens
- ☐ c. Three units
- ☐ d. Three tenths

68 What is the next prime number after 7?

- ☐ a. 9
- ☐ b. 10
- ☐ c. 13
- ☐ d. 11

69 What are the prime factors of 42?

- ☐ a. 6, 7
- ☐ b. 2, 7
- ☐ c. 2, 3, 7
- ☐ d. 1, 6, 7

70 What is the name given to a number which has only two factors?

- ☐ a. Prime
- ☐ b. Odd
- ☐ c. Square
- ☐ d. Even

71 Which of these is not a prime number?

- ☐ a. 29
- ☐ b. 31
- ☐ c. 27
- ☐ d. 23

72 Three cakes cost £1.20. How much will five of the same cakes cost?

- ☐ a. £6
- ☐ b. £3.60
- ☐ c. £2.40
- ☐ d. £2

73 Sam exchanges £40 for 500 French francs (Ff). How many French francs would he get for £100?

- ☐ a. 1,250 Ff
- ☐ b. 5,000 Ff
- ☐ c. 4,000 Ff
- ☐ d. 2,000 Ff

74 A chocolate bar costs 24p. How much do three of these bars cost?

- ☐ a. £2.40
- ☐ b. £0.08
- ☐ c. £0.48
- ☐ d. £0.72

75 A pencil costs 7p. What is the cost of eight pencils?

- ☐ a. 56p
- ☐ b. 54p
- ☐ c. 50p
- ☐ d. 78p

76 A fruit grower employs 12 fruit pickers who pick all of the fruit in 20 days. How many days would it have taken them to pick the fruit if the grower had employed three more pickers?

- ☐ a. 15
- ☐ b. 16
- ☐ c. 14
- ☐ d. 17

77 The cost of hiring a car is £17.00 per day plus a charge of 5p for every mile travelled. What is the cost of hiring a car for five days, travelling a total distance of 1,243 miles?

- ☐ a. £63.00
- ☐ b. £62.32
- ☐ c. £706.50
- ☐ d. £147.15

78 Packets of breakfast cereal are available in four sizes. Which size is the best value?

- ☐ a. 425 g for £2.45
- ☐ b. 500 g for £3.05
- ☐ c. 300 g for £1.77
- ☐ d. 200 g for £1.20

79 When £90.00 is shared in the ratio 1:2, what is the value of the larger share?

- ☐ a. £30.00
- ☐ b. £67.50
- ☐ c. £60.00
- ☐ d. £45.00

80 A recipe for sweet pastry that serves four people contains 200 g of flour, 50 g of sugar, and 2 eggs. How much sugar would you need to use this recipe to serve six people?

- ☐ a. 150 g
- ☐ b. 75 g
- ☐ c. 200 g
- ☐ d. 25 g

81 What is the reciprocal of 5?

- ☐ a. 25
- ☐ b. $\frac{1}{5}$
- ☐ c. 0.5
- ☐ d. $\sqrt{5}$

82 What is the reciprocal of x^2?

- ☐ a. $\frac{1}{x^2}$
- ☐ b. $-x$
- ☐ c. $\sqrt{x}$
- ☐ d. x

83 How do you write the number seventeen thousand and forty eight in figures?

- ☐ a. 1700048
- ☐ b. 170048
- ☐ c. 1748
- ☐ d. 17048

84 Estimate the value of 187×41

- ☐ a. 4,000
- ☐ b. 5,000
- ☐ c. 8,000
- ☐ d. 10,000

85 Write 2.3649 correct to three significant figures.

- ☐ a. 2.365
- ☐ b. 2.37
- ☐ c. 2.36
- ☐ d. 2.4

86 Write 13,781 to the nearest hundred.

- ☐ a. 800
- ☐ b. 14,000
- ☐ c. 13,700
- ☐ d. 13,800

87 Multiply out the brackets and simplify $(\sqrt{3} + \sqrt{2})^2$

- ☐ a. $11 + 2\sqrt{6}$
- ☐ b. 6
- ☐ c. $5 + 2\sqrt{6}$
- ☐ d. 5

Handling data

88 Find the mean of 7, 3, 2, 5, 7, and 6.

- ☐ a. 5
- ☐ b. 5.5
- ☐ c. 30
- ☐ d. 3.5

89 The mean age of three girls is 14. One girl is 17 years old and another is 13 years old. How old is the third girl?

- ☐ a. 12
- ☐ b. 10
- ☐ c. 15
- ☐ d. 14

90 What is used in statistics to measure the spread of a set of data around its median?

- ☐ a. Range
- ☐ b. Interquartile range
- ☐ c. Standard deviation
- ☐ d. Correlation

91 Which word is used to describe the statistic you get by subtracting the smallest value from the largest value of a set of data?

- ☐ a. The median
- ☐ b. The mode
- ☐ c. The mean
- ☐ d. The range

92 What is the name given to a diagram which represents frequencies as sectors of a circle?

- ☐ a. A frequency polygon
- ☐ b. A pie chart
- ☐ c. A bar chart
- ☐ d. A histogram

93 What is used in statistics to measure the spread of a set of data around its mean?

- ☐ a. Correlation
- ☐ b. Standard deviation
- ☐ c. Interquartile range
- ☐ d. The average

94 Find the median of 8, 11, 17, 5, 18, 2, 9.

- ☐ a. 9
- ☐ b. 10
- ☐ c. 5
- ☐ d. 8.5

95 What name is given to the value which occurs most frequently in a set of data?

- ☐ a. The mode
- ☐ b. The mean
- ☐ c. The range
- ☐ d. The median

96 What is the lowest common multiple of 5 and 20?

- ☐ a. 5
- ☐ b. 40
- ☐ c. 100
- ☐ d. 20

97 An unbiased coin is spun at the same time as a fair dice is rolled. How many possible outcomes are there?

- ☐ a. 12
- ☐ b. 6
- ☐ c. 8
- ☐ d. 24

98 A bag contains five identical beads; three are red and two are yellow. One bead is taken from the bag and its colour is noted before it is returned to the bag. Another bead is then taken. What is the probability that the beads taken from the bag are the same colour?

a. $\frac{1}{2}$

b. $\frac{12}{25}$

c. $\frac{9}{25}$

d. $\frac{13}{25}$

99 Two unbiased dice are rolled at the same time. What is the probability that they both show prime numbers when they land?

a. $\frac{1}{3}$

b. $\frac{3}{4}$

c. $\frac{4}{9}$

d. $\frac{1}{4}$

100 A bag contains 26 identical discs each with a different letter of the alphabet on it. When a disc is drawn from the bag, what is the probability that the letter shown is one of the letters in the word MATHEMATICS?

a. $\frac{9}{26}$

b. $\frac{10}{26}$

c. $\frac{11}{26}$

d. $\frac{8}{26}$

101 There are ten chocolates in a box. Four of them are plain and the rest are milk. You pick one without looking and eat it. You pick a second chocolate without looking and eat it. What is the probability that you ate two plain chocolates?

a. $\frac{1}{2}$

b. $\frac{4}{30}$

c. $\frac{1}{5}$

d. $\frac{3}{25}$

102 The probability that a certain car will pass its MOT test is $\frac{11}{16}$. What is the probability that this car will fail its MOT test?

a. $\frac{11}{16}$

b. $\frac{1}{2}$

c. 1

d. $\frac{5}{16}$

Shape and measures

103 Which word is used to describe the total distance around the outside of a shape?

a. Volume
b. Circumference
c. Area
d. Perimeter

104 What is the area of a rectangle which is 4 cm long and 3 cm wide?

a. 7 sq cm
b. 12 sq cm
c. 10 sq cm
d. 14 sq cm

105 How many sides has a triangle?

a. 1
b. 2
c. 3
d. 4

106 What is the name given to a flat shape which can be folded to make a hollow three dimensional solid?

☐ a. An area
☐ b. A scale drawing
☐ c. A volume
☐ d. A net

107 A triangle has an angle of 30° and another angle of 45°. What is the size of the third angle?

☐ a. 180°
☐ b. 45°
☐ c. 90°
☐ d. 105°

108 What is the area of a circle, to two decimal places, whose radius is 12 cm?

☐ a. 1421.12 cm²
☐ b. 452.16 cm²
☐ c. 452.39 cm²
☐ d. 75.40 cm²

109 A rectangle has an area of 48 sq cm. Its length is 8 cm. What is its width?

☐ a. 6 cm
☐ b. 7 cm
☐ c. 8 cm
☐ d. 384 cm

110 Write due west as a three-figure bearing.

☐ a. 090
☐ b. 270
☐ c. 180
☐ d. 360

111 What is the formula for the circumference of a circle?

☐ a. $2\pi r$
☐ b. πr^2
☐ c. $2r$
☐ d. πr

112 What number do you always get when you divide the circumference of a circle by its diameter?

☐ a. 3
☐ b. 2
☐ c. 1
☐ d. π

113 What is the formula for the curved surface area of a cylinder?

☐ a. $2\pi rh$
☐ b. $2\pi r^2 + 2\pi rh$
☐ c. $\pi r^2 h$
☐ d. $2\pi r^2$

114 What is the length of the arc, to the nearest centimetre, subtended by an angle of 110° in a circle of radius 15 cm?

☐ a. 216 cm
☐ b. 110 cm
☐ c. 14 cm
☐ d. 29 cm

115 What is the area, to the nearest square metre, of the sector of a circle of radius 3 m subtended by an angle of 200°?

☐ a. 18 m²
☐ b. 16 m²
☐ c. 10 m²
☐ d. 5 m²

116 What is the diameter of a circle whose radius is 4.8 cm?

- ☐ a. 9.6 cm
- ☐ b. 23.04 cm
- ☐ c. 2.4 cm
- ☐ d. 14.4 cm

117 A car travels at an average speed of 50 kph for two and a half hours. How far has it gone?

- ☐ a. 150 km
- ☐ b. 25 km
- ☐ c. 50 km
- ☐ d. 125 km

118 A lorry travels 300 km at an average speed of 60 kph then travels at an average speed of 25 kph for two hours. What is its average speed for the whole journey?

- ☐ a. 50 kph
- ☐ b. 42.5 kph
- ☐ c. 65 kph
- ☐ d. 85 kph

119 A point P has coordinates $(-3, 3)$. What are its polar coordinates?

- ☐ a. $(3\sqrt{2}, 225°)$
- ☐ b. $(18, 225°)$
- ☐ c. $(3\sqrt{2}, 135°)$
- ☐ d. $(2\sqrt{3}, 135°)$

120 What is the gradient of the straight line graph whose equation is $y = 2x - 3$?

- ☐ a. -3
- ☐ b. 2
- ☐ c. 3
- ☐ d. 0.5

121 What is the intercept of the graph whose equation is $3y - x = 12$?

- ☐ a. 12
- ☐ b. 4
- ☐ c. 3
- ☐ d. -1

122 When a shape is enlarged by a scale factor -3, how are the angles in the new shape related to those in the original shape?

- ☐ a. Three times bigger
- ☐ b. All 3° less
- ☐ c. Three times smaller
- ☐ d. Stay the same

123 What word is used to describe two lines which meet each other at 90°?

- ☐ a. Perpendicular
- ☐ b. Straight
- ☐ c. Tangents
- ☐ d. Parallel

124 Which word is used to describe two lines in the same plane which never meet?

- ☐ a. Parallel
- ☐ b. Perpendicular
- ☐ c. Arcs
- ☐ d. Bisectors

125 Approximately how many centimetres are there in one inch?

- ☐ a. 2.5 cm
- ☐ b. 5 cm
- ☐ c. 10 cm
- ☐ d. 2 cm

126 How many kilometres are there in five miles?

- ☐ a. 5
- ☐ b. 6
- ☐ c. 7
- ☐ d. 8

127 I catch a train at 10.53 and arrive at my destination at 14.07. How many hours and minutes did my journey take?

- ☐ a. 3 h 54 min
- ☐ b. 3 h 14 min
- ☐ c. 2 h 14 min
- ☐ d. 4 h 54 min

128 Write quarter to six in the evening as a time using the 24 hour clock.

- ☐ a. 17.45
- ☐ b. 5.45 p.m.
- ☐ c. 6.15
- ☐ d. 05.45

129 A student's height, h, is measured to the nearest centimetre as 160 cm. Within which range of values must the true height lie?

- ☐ a. $159 < h < 161$
- ☐ b. $159.5 < h < 160.4$
- ☐ c. $159.5 < h < 160.5$
- ☐ d. $155 < h < 165$

130 A room is 7 m long and 4 m wide when measured to the nearest metre. If the true area of the room is A, within which range of values will A lie?

- ☐ a. $26.25 < A < 29.25$
- ☐ b. $22.75 < A < 33.75$
- ☐ c. $27 < A < 29$
- ☐ d. $27.5 < A < 28.5$

131 A map has a scale of 1:240000. Two points are 3.6 cm apart on the map. What is the actual distance between these places in kilometres?

- ☐ a. 6.67 km
- ☐ b. 8.64 km
- ☐ c. 0.64 km
- ☐ d. 0.86 km

132 Approximately how many litres are equivalent to one gallon?

- ☐ a. 8
- ☐ b. 2.2
- ☐ c. 5
- ☐ d. 2

133 If you walk at an average speed of 5 kph, how far would you walk in 45 minutes?

- ☐ a. 2.25 km
- ☐ b. 0.1 km
- ☐ c. 3.75 km
- ☐ d. 9 km

134 What is the perimeter of a square whose sides are 5 cm long?

- ☐ a. 10 cm
- ☐ b. 20 cm
- ☐ c. 15 cm
- ☐ d. 25 cm

135 What size is the exterior angle of a regular hexagon?

- ☐ a. 120°
- ☐ b. 45°
- ☐ c. 6°
- ☐ d. 60°

136 What is the sum of the exterior angles of any polygon?

☐ a. 180°
☐ b. 500°
☐ c. 540°
☐ d. 360°

137 The interior angle of a regular polygon is 135°. What shape is this polygon?

☐ a. An octagon
☐ b. A pentagon
☐ c. A heptagon
☐ d. A hexagon

138 How many sides has a pentagon?

☐ a. 5
☐ b. 7
☐ c. 8
☐ d. 6

139 A right-angled triangle has sides 25 cm long and 60 cm long. How long is the hypotenuse?

☐ a. 65 cm
☐ b. 4,225 cm
☐ c. 54.5 cm
☐ d. 85 cm

140 Here are the lengths of the sides of four triangles. Which of them does not have a right angle?

☐ a. 25 m, 60 m, 65 m
☐ b. 5 cm, 12 cm, 13 cm
☐ c. 3 m, 4 m, 5 m
☐ d. 6 cm, 7 cm, 8 cm

141 How many lines of symmetry has a square?

☐ a. 1
☐ b. 2

☐ c. 6
☐ d. 4

142 How many lines of symmetry has a parallelogram?

☐ a. 4
☐ b. 0
☐ c. 2
☐ d. 1

143 What is the name of a quadrilateral which has only one pair of parallel sides?

☐ a. Square
☐ b. Trapezium
☐ c. Parallelogram
☐ d. Rhombus

144 What is the size of the interior angle of a regular pentagon?

☐ a. 108°
☐ b. 90°
☐ c. 72°
☐ d. 135°

145 What day of the week is 1 September if 3 August is a Saturday?

☐ a. Friday
☐ b. Monday
☐ c. Sunday
☐ d. Saturday

146 Which of the following is not a quadrilateral?

☐ a. Rhombus
☐ b. Trapezium
☐ c. Cube
☐ d. Square

147 What is the name of the transformation which involves sliding a shape to its new position?

☐ a. A translation
☐ b. A reflection
☐ c. An enlargement
☐ d. A rotation

148 How many degrees do the three angles in a triangle add up to?

☐ a. 90
☐ b. 180
☐ c. 270
☐ d. 360

149 A right-angled triangle has sides 15 m, 48 m, and 50 m when measured to the nearest metre. Which value could be the tangent of one of its angles?

☐ a. $\frac{24}{25}$

☐ b. $\frac{10}{3}$

☐ c. $\frac{3}{10}$

☐ d. $\frac{5}{16}$

150 Find the volume of a cylinder whose radius is 6 cm and whose height is 12 cm, giving your answer correct to two decimal places.

☐ a. 1357.17 cm³
☐ b. 432.00 cm³
☐ c. 1628.02 cm³
☐ d. 452.39 cm³

151 Work out the volume, in m³, of a cuboid measuring 3 m by 60 cm by 20 cm.

☐ a. 36 m³
☐ b. 360,000 m³

☐ c. 3,600 m³
☐ d. 0.36 m³

152 What is the formula for the volume of a sphere?

☐ a. πr^3

☐ b. $\frac{2}{3}\pi r^3$

☐ c. $\frac{4}{3}\pi r^3$

☐ d. $\frac{3}{4}\pi r^3$

153 What is the volume of a cone whose vertical height is 18 cm and whose base radius is 4 cm, to the nearest cubic centimetre?

☐ a. 302 cm³
☐ b. 288 cm³
☐ c. 1,328 cm³
☐ d. 905 cm³

Biology
Questions

1 Human cells have 46 chromosomes, and cell division by both mitosis and meiosis can occur within the human body. Which of the following shows the correct chromosome number after both mitosis and meiosis take place?

☐ a. mitosis – 46, meiosis – 23
☐ b. mitosis – 46, meiosis – 92
☐ c. mitosis – 92, meiosis – 46
☐ d. mitosis – 23, meiosis – 46

2 Mitochondria are structures within the cell which are responsible for what?

☐ a. Many of the reactions of respiration
☐ b. The control of the cell
☐ c. The reactions of photosynthesis
☐ d. The process of osmosis

3 Cells rarely exist in isolation and are usually grouped together. What is a group of similar cells called?

☐ a. An organ
☐ b. An organism
☐ c. An organ system
☐ d. A tissue

4 Diffusion is the spreading of particles of a gas or any substance in solution by what method?

☐ a. Active movement of particles down a concentration gradient
☐ b. Passive movement of particles down a concentration gradient
☐ c. Passive movement of particles against a concentration gradient
☐ d. Active movement of particles against a concentration gradient

5 Which statement correctly identifies the role of DNA and RNA in the cell?

☐ a. DNA is double-stranded and passes into the cytoplasm, RNA is single-stranded and remains in the nucleus
☐ b. DNA is single-stranded and passes into the cytoplasm, RNA is double-stranded and remains in the nucleus
☐ c. DNA is single-stranded and remains in the nucleus, RNA is double-stranded and passes into the cytoplasm
☐ d. DNA is double-stranded and remains in the nucleus, RNA is single-stranded and passes into the cytoplasm

6 Which one of the following groups of micro-organisms can be used to make foods and drinks?

☐ a. Fungi and viruses
☐ b. Bacteria and fungi
☐ c. Bacteria and viruses
☐ d. Bacteria, fungi, and viruses

7 Enzymes possess which of the following characteristics?

☐ a. They are affected by temperature, are not substrate-specific, and are affected by pH
☐ b. They are affected by temperature, are substrate-specific, and are affected by pH
☐ c. They are affected by temperature, are substrate-specific, and are not affected by pH
☐ d. They are not affected by temperature, are not substrate-specific, and are affected by pH

8 Which of the following features of a bacterial cell are **not** characteristic of plant or animal cells?

☐ a. DNA found in cytoplasm
☐ b. Cytoplasm
☐ c. Cell wall
☐ d. Cell membrane

9 Which tissue has the greatest percentage mass in a typical male and female adult?

☐ a. Fat (essential)
☐ b. Bone
☐ c. Fat (storage)
☐ d. Muscle

10 Which of the following is **not** true for animal cells?

☐ a. No cell wall
☐ b. Small temporary vacuoles
☐ c. No chloroplasts present
☐ d. They have large permanent vacuoles

11 What is osmosis?

☐ a. Movement of water molecules from a region of low concentration to a region of high concentration through a semi-permeable membrane
☐ b. Movement of molecules from a region of low concentration to a region of high concentration
☐ c. Movement of water molecules from a region of high concentration of water molecules to a region of low concentration of water molecules through a semi-permeable membrane
☐ d. Movement of molecules from a region of high concentration to a region of low concentration

Digestion

12 What does the enzyme found in saliva digest?

☐ a. Protein
☐ b. Starch
☐ c. Fats
☐ d. Sugar

13 What is the function of bile?

☐ a. To decrease acidity in the small intestine and digest starch
☐ b. To decrease acidity in the small intestine and emulsify fats

☐ c. To increase acidity in the small
intestine and emulsify fats
☐ d. To decrease acidity in the small
intestine and digest proteins

14 The action of amylase on starch is
to produce simple sugars. This can be
demonstrated by which food test?

☐ a. Biuret test
☐ b. Iodine test
☐ c. Benedict's test
☐ d. None of these

15 How is the small intestine adapted
for absorption?

☐ a. By being long, internally
smooth, and with villi
☐ b. By being long, with internal
folds, and without villi
☐ c. By being long, with internal
folds, and with villi
☐ d. By being short, with internal
folds, and with villi

16 In the digestive system, what is the
function of the colon?

☐ a. It absorbs oxygen from the
indigestible material it
contains
☐ b. It absorbs water from the
indigestible material it
contains
☐ c. It absorbs fibre from the indigestible material it contains
☐ d. It absorbs fat from the indigestible material it contains

17 In the digestive system, what is the
job of the stomach?

☐ a. Emulsification of fats
☐ b. Digestion of fat, protein, and
starch

☐ c. Food storage and digestion of
protein
☐ d. Absorption of water

18 Which enzyme is present in saliva?

☐ a. Prepsin
☐ b. Trypsin
☐ c. Enterokinase
☐ d. Amylase

19 Which of the following is **not** a
property of enzymes?

☐ a. They are made by living cells
☐ b. They are destroyed by heat
☐ c. They are created by heat
☐ d. They are responsible for one
specific reaction

Circulation

20 Arteries and veins have different
functions and therefore they differ in
the thickness of their walls, internal
diameter, and internal structure.
Which statement is true of veins?

☐ a. They have a thinner wall than
arteries, wider internal diameter,
and no valves
☐ b. They have a thicker wall than
arteries, wider internal diameter,
and often contain valves
☐ c. They have a thinner wall than
arteries, narrower internal
diameter, and often contain
valves
☐ d. They have a thinner wall than
arteries, wider internal diameter,
and often contain valves

21 What is the correct direction of blood flow through the heart?

☐ a. Body, left atrium, left ventricle, lungs, right atrium, right ventricle, body
☐ b. Body, right atrium, right ventricle, body, left atrium, left ventricle, lungs
☐ c. Body, right ventricle, right atrium, lungs, left ventricle, left atrium, body
☐ d. Body, right atrium, right ventricle, lungs, left atrium, left ventricle, body

22 What is meant by the double circulatory system?

☐ a. There are two separate hearts, one supplying the lungs, the other supplying the rest of the body
☐ b. Blood flows from the right side of the heart to the lungs, and from the left side of the heart to the rest of the body
☐ c. Blood flows from the left side of the heart to the lungs, and from the right side of the heart to the rest of the body
☐ d. Blood flows from the right side of the heart to the left side of the heart, and from here to the lungs and the rest of the body

23 Which of the following pairs of statements about red and white blood cells is correct?

☐ a. Red cells engulf microbes; white cells have a nucleus
☐ b. Red cells have a nucleus; white cells engulf microbes
☐ c. Red cells contain haemoglobin; white cells have a nucleus
☐ d. Red cells carry oxygen; white cells have no nucleus

24 Which of the following statements applies to all arteries?

☐ a. They carry oxygenated blood
☐ b. They carry deoxygenated blood
☐ c. They carry blood to the heart
☐ d. They carry blood from the heart

25 What is a leukocyte?

☐ a. A platelet
☐ b. A white blood cell
☐ c. An erythrocyte
☐ d. A red blood cell

26 What is haemoglobin?

☐ a. A vessel for carrying plasma
☐ b. A vessel for carrying blood
☐ c. Protein for transporting carbon dioxide
☐ d. Protein for transporting oxygen

27 There are three main types of blood vessels: arteries, veins, and capillaries. Which of the following is **not** true for arteries?

☐ a. They have elastic fibres
☐ b. They have a slow blood flow
☐ c. They have a thick wall
☐ d. They have a rapid blood flow

Breathing and respiration

28 What does breathing in involve?

☐ a. Raising the ribs and lowering the diaphragm

b. Raising the ribs and raising the diaphragm

c. Lowering the ribs and lowering the diaphragm

d. Lowering the ribs and raising the diaphragm

29 Which of the following shows (in the right order) how air moves from the atmosphere to the blood?

a. Nose, trachea, bronchioles, bronchi, alveoli, blood capillaries

b. Nose, bronchi, trachea, bronchioles, alveoli, blood capillaries

c. Nose, trachea, bronchi, bronchioles, alveoli, blood capillaries

d. Nose, trachea, bronchi, alveoli, bronchioles, blood capillaries

30 Where does gas exchange in the lungs take place?

a. In the bronchioles
b. In the alveoli
c. In the bronchi
d. In the trachea

31 What is the composition of gases in inhaled and exhaled air?

a. Air in = nitrogen 78%, oxygen 21%, carbon dioxide 0.03%, others 1%. Air out = nitrogen 78%, oxygen 18%, carbon dioxide 3%, others 1%

b. Air in = nitrogen 78%, oxygen 18%, carbon dioxide 3%, others 1%. Air out = nitrogen 78%, oxygen 21%, carbon dioxide 0.03%, others 1%

c. Air in = nitrogen 68%, oxygen 31%, carbon dioxide 0.03%, others 1%. Air out = nitrogen 78%, oxygen 18%, carbon dioxide 3%, others 1%

d. Air in = nitrogen 78%, oxygen 21%, carbon dioxide 0.03%, others 1%. Air out = nitrogen 76%, oxygen 20%, carbon dioxide 3%, others 1%

32 What does the process of aerobic respiration require?

a. Carbon dioxide
b. Oxygen
c. Water
d. Heat

33 When does fermentation occur?

a. Yeast respires, producing oxygen and alcohol

b. Yeast respires, producing carbon dioxide and alcohol

c. Yeast respires, producing carbon dioxide and lactic acid

d. Yeast respires, producing lactic acid and alcohol

34 When there is a lack of oxygen in the muscles anaerobic respiration occurs, which leads to the accumulation of a substance that causes muscle fatigue. What is this substance called?

a. Water
b. Glucose
c. Lactic acid
d. Carbon dioxide

35 When yeasts respire without oxygen, what is the process called?

- ☐ a. Photosynthesis
- ☐ b. Excretion
- ☐ c. Aerobic respiration
- ☐ d. Anaerobic respiration

36 Which of the following substances produced by yeast during anaerobic respiration (fermentation) is useful in breadmaking?

- ☐ a. Oxygen and ethanol (alcohol)
- ☐ b. Carbon dioxide and ethanol (alcohol)
- ☐ c. Oxygen
- ☐ d. Carbon dioxide

Nervous system

37 On its way to the retina at the back of the eye, light does **not** pass through which structure?

- ☐ a. The pupil
- ☐ b. The cornea
- ☐ c. The ciliary muscles
- ☐ d. The lens

38 All organisms respond to changes in their surroundings, and this response involves a certain sequence of events. Which of the following sequences is true?

- ☐ a. Stimulus → receptor → coordination → effector → response
- ☐ b. Stimulus → effector → coordination → receptor → response
- ☐ c. Stimulus → coordination → receptor → effector → response

- ☐ d. Stimulus → receptor → effector → coordination → response

39 Which of the following stimuli do receptors detect?

- ☐ a. Light, sound, pressure, temperature, and metabolism
- ☐ b. Light, sound, pressure, temperature, and chemicals
- ☐ c. Light, sound, temperature, chemicals, and photosynthesis
- ☐ d. Light, sound, pressure, temperature, and respiration

40 Which of the following structures help to produce a focused image on the retina?

- ☐ a. The lens and cornea
- ☐ b. The lens and fovea
- ☐ c. The lens and blind spot
- ☐ d. The lens and optic nerve

41 Which of the following shows the correct sequence for the pathway of nervous impulses in a reflex arc?

- ☐ a. Receptor → relay neurone → sensory neurone → motor neurone → effector
- ☐ b. Receptor → motor neurone → relay neurone → sensory neurone → effector
- ☐ c. Receptor → sensory neurone → motor neurone → relay neurone → effector
- ☐ d. Receptor → sensory neurone → relay neurone → motor neurone → effector

42 Which part of the brain is responsible for the control of balance?

- [ ] a. The cerebrum
- [ ] b. The medulla
- [ ] c. The cerebellum
- [ ] d. None of these

43 To focus the light from near or distant objects, in what way does the shape of the lens alter?

- [ ] a. By contraction and relaxation of the suspensory ligaments
- [ ] b. By contraction or relaxation of the ciliary muscles
- [ ] c. By contraction and relaxation of the iris
- [ ] d. By contraction and relaxation of the optic nerve

Hormones

44 Which hormones, involved in the menstrual cycle of women, are **not** produced by the pituitary gland?

- [ ] a. Oestrogen and lutenizing hormone
- [ ] b. Oestrogen and progesterone
- [ ] c. Progesterone and lutenizing hormone
- [ ] d. Oestrogen and follicle-stimulating hormone

45 Compared to the action of nerves, which of the following is true about hormones?

- [ ] a. They travel slower and have a longer-lasting response
- [ ] b. They travel quicker and have a shorter-lasting response
- [ ] c. They travel slower and have a shorter-lasting response

- [ ] d. They travel quicker and have a longer-lasting response

46 Which hormone can be used as a fertility drug?

- [ ] a. Lutenizing hormone
- [ ] b. Progesterone
- [ ] c. Follicle-stimulating hormone
- [ ] d. Oestrogen

47 If the blood glucose level is too low, which hormone converts glycogen to glucose?

- [ ] a. Oestrogen
- [ ] b. Insulin
- [ ] c. Antidiuretic hormone
- [ ] d. Glucagon

48 Where in the body is insulin normally produced?

- [ ] a. In the liver
- [ ] b. In the colon
- [ ] c. In the pancreas
- [ ] d. In the duodenum

49 What condition is treated by injections of insulin into the abdomen?

- [ ] a. Kidney failure
- [ ] b. Diabetes mellitus
- [ ] c. Pancreatitis
- [ ] d. Duodenal ulcer

50 What is insulin?

- [ ] a. An enzyme
- [ ] b. A gene
- [ ] c. A pigment
- [ ] d. A hormone

Homeostasis

51 If the body becomes too cold which action decreases blood flow to the skin?

- ☐ a. Increased liver action
- ☐ b. Vasoconstriction
- ☐ c. Shivering
- ☐ d. Vasodilation

52 What is the removal of metabolic wastes from cells called?

- ☐ a. Secretion
- ☐ b. Excretion
- ☐ c. Egestion
- ☐ d. Respiration

53 If the body is becoming dehydrated which of the following statements is true?

- ☐ a. Less antidiuretic hormone is released, causing the kidneys to reabsorb more water
- ☐ b. More antidiuretic hormone is released, causing the kidneys to reabsorb less water
- ☐ c. More antidiuretic hormone is released, causing the kidneys to reabsorb more water
- ☐ d. Less antidiuretic hormone is released, causing the kidneys to reabsorb less water

54 How is excess blood sugar stored when a body is at rest?

- ☐ a. Glucose is changed into glycogen and stored in the pancreas
- ☐ b. Glycogen is changed into glucose and stored in the liver and muscles
- ☐ c. Glucose is changed into glycogen and stored in the liver and muscles
- ☐ d. Glycogen is changed into glucose and stored in the pancreas

55 Which organ is responsible for urea formation?

- ☐ a. The colon
- ☐ b. The ileum
- ☐ c. The kidneys
- ☐ d. The liver

56 The liver is an important homeostatic organ. What does 'homeostasis' mean?

- ☐ a. The process by which undigested waste is eliminated from the body
- ☐ b. The removal from the body of the waste products of cell metabolism
- ☐ c. The process by which a constant balance of osmotic pressure is maintained
- ☐ d. The maintenance of a constant internal environment, despite changes in the external environment

57 During exercise, why does the body attempt to lose more energy?

- ☐ a. To keep the body cool
- ☐ b. To keep the body temperature constant
- ☐ c. To keep the body warm
- ☐ d. To keep blood pressure down

58 The Bowman's capsule contains glucose but the loop of Henle does not. Why?

- ☐ a. It has been secreted by the Bowman's capsule
- ☐ b. It has been reabsorbed by the second convoluted tubule
- ☐ c. It has been reabsorbed into the blood
- ☐ d. It has been secreted by the ureter

59 Which of the following is **not** an organ of excretion in mammals?

- ☐ a. The liver
- ☐ b. The skin
- ☐ c. The lungs
- ☐ d. The stomach

Health

60 Which of the following substances is **not** a drug?

- ☐ a. An enzyme
- ☐ b. A solvent
- ☐ c. A hallucinogen
- ☐ d. A stimulant

61 What effect does drinking too much alcohol have?

- ☐ a. Improves judgement and damages the liver and brain
- ☐ b. Impairs judgement but does not harm the liver and brain
- ☐ c. Does not impair judgement and does not harm liver or brain
- ☐ d. Impairs judgement and damages the liver and brain

62 What negative effects does smoking have?

- ☐ a. Damages the lungs and heart but does not harm the blood vessels
- ☐ b. Damages the lungs but does not harm the heart or blood vessels
- ☐ c. Damages the lungs, heart, and blood vessels
- ☐ d. Does not damage the lungs, heart, or blood vessels

63 Which one of the following is **not** a defence against the entry of infective micro-organisms?

- ☐ a. Skin
- ☐ b. Blood clots
- ☐ c. White blood cells
- ☐ d. Mucus

64 Antibiotics are medicines that help to cure disease caused by what?

- ☐ a. Viruses inside the body cells
- ☐ b. Bacteria inside the body but not inside the body cells
- ☐ c. Bacteria on the surface of the skin
- ☐ d. Bacteria inside the body cells

65 What does active immunization involve?

- ☐ a. The introduction of a living form of a pathogen into the body, resulting in antigen production
- ☐ b. The introduction of an inactive or dead form of a pathogen into the body, resulting in antigen production
- ☐ c. The introduction of an inactive or dead form of a pathogen into the body, resulting in antibody production

d. The introduction of a living pathogen into the body, resulting in antibody production

66 Which of the following statements is **not** true about how white blood cells defend the body against infective micro-organisms?

☐ a. They help blood to clot
☐ b. They produce antibodies
☐ c. They produce antitoxins
☐ d. They ingest micro-organisms

67 Which one of the following statements is **not** true about preventing the increasing resistance of bacteria to antibiotics?

☐ a. Antibiotics should not be overused
☐ b. Antibiotics should not be used at all
☐ c. New antibiotics should be continually developed
☐ d. Antibiotics should be used as much as possible

68 The immune response involves which of the following blood cells?

☐ a. B cells, red cells, and memory cells
☐ b. Red cells and memory cells
☐ c. B cells and T cells
☐ d. B cells, T cells, and memory cells

69 Which of the following statements about viruses is correct?

☐ a. Viruses are smaller than bacteria, have a nucleus, and are non-living
☐ b. Viruses are smaller than bacteria, have no nucleus, and are non-living

☐ c. Viruses are larger than bacteria, have no nucleus, and are non-living
☐ d. Viruses are smaller than bacteria, have no nucleus, and are living

70 A kidney machine works on the principle of dialysis. What is the process by which substances pass from the dialysis tubing into the solution?

☐ a. Defraction
☐ b. Diffusion
☐ c. Osmosis
☐ d. Filtration

Movement

71 Which of the following structures of a joint best fits this description: 'has tensile strength and some elasticity'?

☐ a. Ligament
☐ b. Tendon
☐ c. Synovial membrane
☐ d. Cartilage

72 The knee joint is the largest and most complex joint in the human body. It is similar to a hinge joint but with a slight rotation that allows the leg to lock into a rigid position when extended. What does the synovial fluid do?

☐ a. It helps to protect the patella
☐ b. It reduces friction between the bones
☐ c. It reduces friction between the ligaments and muscles
☐ d. It prevents the joint overextending

73 What does a ligament do?

☐ a. It holds bones of a joint together
☐ b. It lubricates a joint to reduce friction
☐ c. It reduces friction between bones at a joint
☐ d. It connects muscle to a bone

74 What is the job of a tendon?

☐ a. To connect muscle to a bone
☐ b. To lubricate a joint to reduce friction
☐ c. To hold bones of a joint together
☐ d. To reduce friction between bones at a joint

75 What does cartilage do?

☐ a. It reduces friction between bones of a joint
☐ b. It connects muscle to a bone
☐ c. It holds bones of a joint together
☐ d. It lubricates a joint to reduce friction

Reproduction

76 Which is the correct pathway taken by a sperm cell from its place of production in one of the testes to where it will fertilize an egg?

☐ a. testis → sperm duct → urethra → vagina → oviduct → uterus
☐ b. testis → sperm duct → urethra → uterus → vagina → oviduct
☐ c. testis → urethra → sperm duct → vagina → uterus → oviduct
☐ d. testis → sperm duct → urethra → vagina → uterus → oviduct

77 Which structure in the human female produces the eggs?

☐ a. The oviduct
☐ b. The urethra
☐ c. The uterus
☐ d. The ovary

78 What protects the developing foetus from physical damage?

☐ a. Plasma
☐ b. Amniotic fluid
☐ c. Tissue fluid
☐ d. Fat

79 What does the placenta supply the foetus with?

☐ a. Food and carbon dioxide
☐ b. Urea and oxygen
☐ c. Urea and carbon dioxide
☐ d. Food and oxygen

Green plants as organisms

80 The sugars produced by photosynthesis are used in which of the following ways?

☐ a. To make starch for storage, cellulose for support, and in respiration for energy production
☐ b. To make starch for energy production, cellulose for support, and in respiration for storage
☐ c. To make cellulose for storage, starch for support, and in respiration for energy production
☐ d. To make cellulose for energy production, starch for support, and in respiration for storage

81 The rate of photosynthesis is limited by which of the following factors?

- ☐ a. Light intensity, carbon dioxide concentration, but not temperature
- ☐ b. Light intensity, but not carbon dioxide concentration, or temperature
- ☐ c. Light intensity, carbon dioxide concentration, and temperature
- ☐ d. Carbon dioxide concentration, temperature, but not light intensity

82 The most important part of the leaf through which gases enter and leave is called what?

- ☐ a. Xylem
- ☐ b. Epidermis
- ☐ c. Cuticle
- ☐ d. Stomata

83 Which of the following structures in the leaf is **not** directly involved with photosynthesis?

- ☐ a. Palisade layer
- ☐ b. Cuticle
- ☐ c. Stomata
- ☐ d. Xylem

84 What three minerals are required by the plant to make proteins, DNA, and chlorophyll (in that order)?

- ☐ a. Phosphorus, nitrogen, and magnesium
- ☐ b. Phosphorus, magnesium, and nitrogen
- ☐ c. Nitrogen, phosphorus, and magnesium
- ☐ d. Magnesium, phosphorus, and nitrogen

85 Plants are sensitive to various stimuli. Which of the following is **not** known to affect plants?

- ☐ a. Gravity
- ☐ b. Sound
- ☐ c. Water
- ☐ d. Light

86 The shoot of a green plant is said to show positive phototropism. In what way does this mean that it grows?

- ☐ a. Towards light
- ☐ b. Towards water
- ☐ c. Away from light
- ☐ d. Towards gravity

87 The hormones which control growth and reproduction in plants can be used for commercial purposes. Which of the following uses is **not** correct?

- ☐ a. They are sprayed on plants to keep them small
- ☐ b. They are used as rooting powder to promote root growth
- ☐ c. They are used on unpollinated flowers to produce 'seedless fruits'
- ☐ d. They are used as selective weedkillers to control broad-leaved weeds

88 What increases the rate of transpiration?

- ☐ a. Increase in temperature, decrease in wind, increase in humidity
- ☐ b. Decrease in temperature, increase in wind, increase in humidity

☐ c. Increase in temperature, increase in wind, decrease in humidity

☐ d. Increase in temperature, decrease in wind, decrease in humidity

89 What transports sugar throughout plants?

☐ a. The epidermis
☐ b. The xylem
☐ c. The phloem
☐ d. The cuticle

90 Which of the following statements is **not** true about the control of plant diseases?

☐ a. Plant diseases can be controlled by selective breeding, chemical treatment, and crop rotation
☐ b. Plant diseases can be controlled by a variety of sowing times, grafting, and crop rotation
☐ c. Plant diseases can be controlled by selective breeding, crop rotation, and fertilizing
☐ d. Plant diseases can be controlled by chemical treatment, grafting, and legislation

91 How are leaves adapted to absorb light?

☐ a. They have bumpy surfaces
☐ b. They are green
☐ c. They have a large surface area
☐ d. They are narrow

92 Why are most chloroplasts found in the palisade layer of a leaf?

☐ a. The palisade layer receives most oxygen
☐ b. The palisade layer receives most water

☐ c. The palisade layer receives most carbon dioxide
☐ d. The palisade layer receives most light

93 Green plants produce carbohydrates by photosynthesis. Which of the following factors does **not** have an effect on the **rate** of photosynthesis?

☐ a. The temperature
☐ b. The size of the leaf surface area
☐ c. The amount of light falling on a plant
☐ d. The amount of nitrogen in the atmosphere

94 Why is the cuticle of a leaf transparent?

☐ a. To allow air through
☐ b. To prevent light entering
☐ c. To allow light through
☐ d. To allow water through

95 Plants and animals generally respond to stimuli in different ways. Which of the following statements is **not** true for plants?

☐ a. Responses are usually slow
☐ b. The effect is usually permanent
☐ c. A short stimulus is usually required
☐ d. Coordination is by hormones only

96 Under what circumstances would you expect stomata to be closed during the day?

☐ a. In very cold conditions
☐ b. In very windy condition
☐ c. In very hot conditions
☐ d. In very bright conditions

97 What is transpiration?

☐ a. A growth movement by part of a plant towards a stimulus
☐ b. Movement of substances about the plant
☐ c. Loss of water vapour to the atmosphere from the surface of the plant
☐ d. The movement of a whole organism in response to a stimulus

98 What is the balanced symbol equation for photosynthesis?

☐ a. $6CO_2 + 6H_2O \rightarrow C_6H_{12}O_6 + 6O_2$
☐ b. $6CO_2 + 6H_2O \rightarrow C_6H_{12}O_6 + 6O$
☐ c. $6CO_2 + 6H_2O \rightarrow C_6 H_2 O_6 + 6O_2$
☐ d. $6O_2 + 6H_2O \rightarrow C_6H_{12}O_6 + 6CO_2$

Variation, classification, and inheritance

99 Which one of the following statements is **not** correct about the formation of recombinant DNA?

☐ a. A desirable gene is removed from a donor chromosome
☐ b. Special restriction and ligase enzymes are used to cut and rejoin the DNA
☐ c. Donor chromosomes are called plasmids
☐ d. The desirable gene is joined onto DNA in bacteria

100 Which of the following statements about the hazards of genetic engineering is **not** correct?

☐ a. The new gene, when inserted into the organism, may affect the function of the other genes
☐ b. The new gene, when recombined, will produce a completely new organism
☐ c. The new gene could enter other organisms not intended for it
☐ d. The new gene, when inserted into a microorganism, could cause it to become dangerous if it 'escapes' into the environment

101 What is a species?

☐ a. A group of organisms that look like each other
☐ b. A group of organisms capable of interbreeding to produce infertile offspring
☐ c. All the organisms present in the animal kingdom
☐ d. A group of organisms capable of interbreeding to produce fertile offspring

102 What are yeasts?

☐ a. Single-celled organisms that have one nucleus, cytoplasm, and no cell wall
☐ b. Single-celled organisms that have one nucleus, cytoplasm, and a cell wall
☐ c. Thread-like organisms that have one nucleus, cytoplasm, and a cell wall
☐ d. Single-celled organisms that have many nuclei, cytoplasm, and a cell wall

103 The binomial system is used as a basis for naming species. Which of the following is the correct way to name the human species using this system?

- ☐ a. homo Sapiens
- ☐ b. homo sapiens
- ☐ c. Sapiens, homo
- ☐ d. Homo sapiens

104 Which of the following observations about evolution is **not** correct?

- ☐ a. All organisms potentially over-reproduce
- ☐ b. Some variations are inherited
- ☐ c. Population numbers change over long periods of time
- ☐ d. Organisms demonstrate variation

105 Which statement about natural selection is **not** correct?

- ☐ a. Individuals with characteristics most suited to the environment are more likely to survive and breed successfully
- ☐ b. Individual organisms within a species usually show no variation
- ☐ c. The genes that have enabled individuals to survive are passed on to the next generation
- ☐ d. Predation, disease, and competition cause large numbers of individuals to die

106 What is a short section of DNA which may be copied and carried on to the next generation called?

- ☐ a. A chromosome
- ☐ b. Cytoplasm
- ☐ c. A gene
- ☐ d. A nucleus

107 What is the sex-chromosome content of a sperm cell?

- ☐ a. Y and Y
- ☐ b. X and Y
- ☐ c. X or Y
- ☐ d. X and X

108 Two heterozygous organisms both with the genotype Bb were crossed. What is the expected ratio of the genotypes of the offspring?

- ☐ a. $\frac{3}{4}$ BB, $\frac{1}{4}$ Bb
- ☐ b. $\frac{1}{3}$ BB, $\frac{1}{3}$ Bb, $\frac{1}{3}$ bb
- ☐ c. $\frac{1}{4}$ BB, $\frac{1}{2}$ Bb, $\frac{1}{4}$ bb
- ☐ d. $\frac{1}{2}$ BB, $\frac{1}{2}$ bb

109 Cystic fibrosis is caused by a recessive allele of a gene, and it can be passed on by both parents even if neither one has the disorder. The parents act as 'carriers' and are heterozygous. If both persons in a couple are carriers for cystic fibrosis, why might they be advised not to have children?

- ☐ a. There is a greater likelihood of the children's genes mutating to produce the disorder
- ☐ b. The children could inherit a recessive gene from each parent and show the disorder
- ☐ c. All their children would be certain to show the disorder
- ☐ d. It is not possible for them to have normal children

110 DNA is made of long strands that have different compounds called bases. How many of these bases are there?

- ☐ a. Five
- ☐ b. Three
- ☐ c. Six
- ☐ d. Four

111 What does selective breeding involve?

- ☐ a. Selecting parents with any traits, crossing them, selecting from their offspring, and repeating the process over several generations
- ☐ b. Selecting parents with desirable traits, crossing them, using all their offspring, and repeating the process over several generations
- ☐ c. Selecting parents with desirable traits, crossing them, selecting from their offspring, and repeating the process over several generations
- ☐ d. Selecting parents with desirable traits, crossing them, selecting from their offspring, and repeating the process over one or two generations

112 What effect does selective breeding have on the numbers of alleles in a population?

- ☐ a. It increases their number
- ☐ b. It sometimes decreases their number
- ☐ c. It decreases their number
- ☐ d. It sometimes increases their number

113 What is the term for producing genetically identical copies of plants or animals?

- ☐ a. Sexual reproduction
- ☐ b. Evolution
- ☐ c. Cloning
- ☐ d. Natural selection

114 Mutations are a source of genetic variation. Which of the following is the most accurate statement about them?

- ☐ a. Some mutations are useful and some are harmful
- ☐ b. All mutations are harmful
- ☐ c. Some mutations are useful but most are harmful
- ☐ d. Most mutations are useful

115 Why is sexual reproduction a source of genetic variation?

- ☐ a. It involves the random fusion of gametes produced by meiosis
- ☐ b. It involves the non-random fusion of gametes produced by mitosis
- ☐ c. It involves the random fusion of gametes produced by mitosis
- ☐ d. It involves the non-random fusion of gametes produced by meiosis

116 DNA is a molecule containing a number of alleles arranged lengthwise. Where do you find DNA inside a cell?

- ☐ a. Inside chloroplasts within the nucleus
- ☐ b. Inside chromosomes within the nucleus
- ☐ c. Inside chromosomes within the cytoplasm
- ☐ d. Inside chloroplasts within the cytoplasm

117 What does homozygous mean?

☐ a. A condition where a pair of identical alleles occurs in the same cell
☐ b. A condition where corresponding chromosomes are inherited from male and female parents
☐ c. A condition where a pair of contrasting alleles occurs in the same cell
☐ d. A condition where contrasting chromosomes are inherited from male and female parents

118 What does heterozygous mean?

☐ a. A condition where a pair of identical alleles occurs in the same cell
☐ b. A condition where corresponding chromosomes are inherited from male and female parents
☐ c. A condition where a pair of contrasting alleles occurs in the same cell
☐ d. A condition where contrasting chromosomes are inherited from male and female parents

119 What is an allele?

☐ a. An alternative form of a gene occupying the same place on a chromosome and affecting the same characteristic but in different ways
☐ b. The number of chromosomes found in body cells made up of homologous pairs
☐ c. The structure in the chromosome which determines hereditary characteristics
☐ d. A single set of chromosomes

Living things in their environment

120 Polar bears are adapted for living in arctic conditions. Which of the following adaptations is **not** correct?

☐ a. There is a thick hairy coat
☐ b. There is no layer of body fat
☐ c. They have a large size and compact shape
☐ d. The feet are not small

121 What are animals that kill and eat other animals called?

☐ a. Predators
☐ b. Prey
☐ c. Decomposers
☐ d. Producers

122 What are organisms that make food called?

☐ a. Decomposers
☐ b. Consumers
☐ c. Producers
☐ d. Herbivores

123 Which statement about the pyramid of biomass is true?

☐ a. The mass of secondary consumers is more than the mass of primary consumers
☐ b. The mass of tertiary consumers is more than the mass of secondary consumers
☐ c. The mass of producers is less than the mass of primary consumers
☐ d. The mass of secondary consumers is less than the mass of primary consumers

124 As energy flows through an ecosystem it is changed from one form to another. Which of the following represents the correct sequence?

☐ a. Heat energy → light energy → chemical energy
☐ b. Light energy → heat energy → chemical energy
☐ c. Chemical energy → light energy → heat energy
☐ d. Light energy → chemical energy → heat energy

125 Which of the following statements about improving the efficiency of food production is **not** correct?

☐ a. Limit the movement of food animals
☐ b. Grow individual plants as close together as possible
☐ c. Control the temperature of the surroundings of food animals
☐ d. Make the food chain as short as possible

126 Which organisms break down the dead bodies of other organisms in ecosystems?

☐ a. Carnivores
☐ b. Producers
☐ c. Herbivores
☐ d. Decomposers

127 When fossil fuels are burned, which of the following gases released is responsible for acid rain?

☐ a. Carbon dioxide
☐ b. Water vapour
☐ c. Sulphur dioxide
☐ d. Carbon monoxide

128 What do human activities pollute?

☐ a. Water, air, and land
☐ b. Water and land, not air
☐ c. Water only
☐ d. Water and air, not land

129 The greenhouse effect is thought to be caused by increasing amounts of which of the following gases?

☐ a. Carbon dioxide and sulphur dioxide
☐ b. Carbon dioxide and methane
☐ c. Carbon dioxide and nitrogen
☐ d. Carbon dioxide and water vapour

130 Pollution of water by fertilizers may cause eutrophication. What is the final result of this process?

☐ a. Suffocation of fish and other aquatic animals
☐ b. Increased use of oxygen from the water by microorganisms
☐ c. Increase in the number of microorganisms
☐ d. Rapid growth of water plants

131 In the carbon cycle the conversion of carbon from atmosphere → plants → animals → atmosphere is accomplished by which of the following processes (in the correct order)?

☐ a. Photosynthesis, respiration, feeding
☐ b. Respiration, photosynthesis, feeding
☐ c. Photosynthesis, feeding, respiration
☐ d. Feeding, photosynthesis, respiration

132 Which of the following statements about how nitrogen is converted during the nitrogen cycle is **not** correct?

☐ a. Nitrogen is converted from ammonia to nitrates by nitrifying bacteria
☐ b. Nitrogen is converted from nitrates to nitrogen gas by denitrifying bacteria
☐ c. Atmospheric nitrogen is changed into nitrates by nitrogen-fixing bacteria
☐ d. Nitrogen is converted from nitrates to nitrogen gas by nitrifying bacteria

133 What is the term for living things interacting with each other and their environment?

☐ a. A food web
☐ b. An ecosystem
☐ c. A habitat
☐ d. A community

134 Which statement is **not** true about the shape and structures that adapt birds for flight?

☐ a. Zig-zag arrangement of muscles that produces wave-like movements of the body
☐ b. Honeycombed bones that reduce weight
☐ c. Streamlined body shape that reduces resistance during flight
☐ d. Wings that provide a large surface area for downward push

135 Which statement is **not** true about the shape and structures that adapt fish for swimming?

☐ a. Median fins that keep the fish upright
☐ b. Paired fins that enable downward and backward movement
☐ c. A gas-filled swim-bladder that provides buoyancy
☐ d. An aerofoil shape that generates lift while swimming

136 Micro-organisms can be grown on a large scale in containers called fermenters. Which of the following characteristics about these fermenters is **not** correct?

☐ a. They have a water-cooled jacket
☐ b. They have temperature and pH monitors
☐ c. They are open to the air
☐ d. They possess stirrers

137 To obtain the sterile conditions needed when growing and handling microorganisms, what actions are taken?

☐ a. Boiling/steaming glass petri dishes, washing inoculating loops, and sealing petri-dish lids
☐ b. Washing glass petri dishes, flaming inoculating loops, and sealing petri-dish lids
☐ c. Boiling/steaming glass petri dishes, flaming inoculating loops, and not sealing petri-dish lids
☐ d. Boiling/steaming glass petri dishes, flaming inoculating loops, and sealing petri-dish lids

138 By which method can food **not** be kept for a long time?

☐ a. Canning it
☐ b. Storing it in a freezer
☐ c. Storing it in a refrigerator
☐ d. Drying it

139 Adding sugar or salt to a food can be used as a basis for food preservation. What does it result in?

☐ a. A decrease in solute concentration and a decrease in water potential of the food
☐ b. An increase in solute concentration and an increase in water potential of the food
☐ c. An increase in solute concentration and decrease in water potential of the food
☐ d. A decrease in solute concentration and an increase in water potential of the food

140 Which of the following statements about feeding in mosquitoes, aphids, houseflies, and butterflies is true?

☐ a. They feed by absorbing already digested food over the whole body surface
☐ b. They feed by biting off pieces of food and chewing them
☐ c. They feed by sucking fluids into their mouth
☐ d. They feed by filtering particles

141 What type of organism is a parasite?

☐ a. One that lives in or on another living organism and obtains food from it

☐ b. One that lives in or on another living organism and both exchange food materials with each other
☐ c. One that lives in or on another dead organism and obtains food from it
☐ d. One that lives in or on another living organism and provides food for it

142 In carnivores what are the correct functions for the following teeth types?

☐ a. Incisors = cutting; canines = shearing; premolars, molars = piercing
☐ b. Incisors = cutting; canines = piercing; premolars, molars = shearing
☐ c. Incisors = shearing; canines = piercing; premolars, molars = cutting
☐ d. Incisors = piercing; canines = cutting; premolars, molars = shearing

143 Sheep and cows are animals with which of the following characteristics?

☐ a. Do not have a rumen and re-chew partly digested food from the stomach
☐ b. Have a rumen between the oesophagus and the stomach and do not re-chew partly digested food from the rumen
☐ c. Have a rumen between the stomach and intestines and re-chew partly digested food from the rumen
☐ d. Have a rumen between the oesophagus and stomach and re-chew partly digested food from the rumen

144 What is the term for the relationship between herbivores and cellulose-digesting bacteria living inside them?

☐ a. Mutualism
☐ b. Parasitism
☐ c. Predation
☐ d. Competition

145 Here are four organisms in a food chain. Which one is a producer?

☐ a. Small molluscs
☐ b. Osprey
☐ c. Algae
☐ d. Flounder

146 In a food chain consisting of algae, small molluscs, flounder, and osprey, which one is a primary consumer?

☐ a. Small molluscs
☐ b. Flounder
☐ c. Algae
☐ d. Osprey

147 Which marine plants, like seaweed, help combat global warming by removing carbon dioxide from the atmosphere during photosynthesis?

☐ a. Plankton
☐ b. Mangrove
☐ c. Algae
☐ d. Corals

148 Which word accurately describes things that are capable of being broken down by living organisms?

☐ a. Biodiversity
☐ b. Biochemical
☐ c. Biological
☐ d. Biodegradable

149 How would fish die if oxygen levels fall?

☐ a. Heat stroke
☐ b. Suffocation
☐ c. Fin rot
☐ d. Exhaustion

150 What is the name for the local environment in which an organism lives, and which provides most of its needs?

☐ a. Habitat
☐ b. Settlement
☐ c. Ecosystem
☐ d. Vicinity

Chemistry Questions

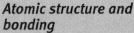

Atomic structure and bonding

1 What term is used for different atoms of the same element?

- ☐ a. Isotope
- ☐ b. Isomer
- ☐ c. Allotrope
- ☐ d. Monomer

2 What is the electron arrangement in the boron atom?

- ☐ a. 5
- ☐ b. 3.2
- ☐ c. 2.3
- ☐ d. 2.2.1

3 Carbon-14 decays with a half-life of 5,730 years. Which of the following statements is true?

- ☐ a. 5,730 atoms decay in one year
- ☐ b. 5,730 atoms decay per second
- ☐ c. On average, half of the carbon-14 atoms change to nitrogen in 5,730 years
- ☐ d. Every 5,730 years a carbon atom decays

4 The physical characteristics of substances depend on the type of chemical bonds in the substances. Bonds can be ionic or covalent. Which of the following statements is the only one that is **true** for covalent compounds?

- ☐ a. They always contain a metal
- ☐ b. They never have a smell
- ☐ c. They are non-electrolytes
- ☐ d. They are hard, crystalline solids

5 What does the electrolysis of brine (sodium chloride solution) produce?

- ☐ a. Sodium hydroxide, hydrogen, and chlorine
- ☐ b. Sodium hydride and chlorine
- ☐ c. Sodium hydroxide and chlorine
- ☐ d. Sodium chlorate and hydrogen

6 Which of the following represents the charge and mass of an electron?

- ☐ a. Charge -1 and mass 1/1840 units
- ☐ b. Charge -1 and mass 1 unit
- ☐ c. Charge $+1$ and mass 1 unit
- ☐ d. Charge $+1$ and mass 1/1840 units

7 Which of the following describes the structure of an atom of lithium (mass number 7 and atomic number 3)?

- [ ] a. 4 electrons, 4 protons, and 3 neutrons
- [ ] b. 3 electrons, 4 protons, and 4 neutrons
- [ ] c. 3 electrons, 3 protons, and 4 neutrons
- [ ] d. 3 electrons, 3 protons, and 7 neutrons

8 Which of the following does the atomic number indicate?

- [ ] a. The number of neutrons only and the period in the periodic table
- [ ] b. The number of electrons and neutrons and the position in the periodic table
- [ ] c. The number of protons or electrons and the position in the periodic table
- [ ] d. The number of protons and neutrons and the group in the periodic table

9 Which of the following would an element in group II have?

- [ ] a. One or two electrons in its outer electron shell
- [ ] b. Two electrons in its outer electron shell
- [ ] c. Only two electrons in the atom
- [ ] d. Six electrons in its outer electron shell

10 In order to become stable which of the following must atoms obtain?

- [ ] a. A positive charge
- [ ] b. Two or more electrons in their outer shells
- [ ] c. Full outer shells of electrons
- [ ] d. Full first shells of two electrons

11 A metal X reacts to form an X^{2+} particle. Which of the following describes what has occurred?

- [ ] a. X has lost two protons
- [ ] b. X has lost two electrons
- [ ] c. X has gained two electrons
- [ ] d. X has gained two protons

12 What name is used to describe an atom with a charge?

- [ ] a. Ion
- [ ] b. Isomer
- [ ] c. Compound
- [ ] d. Isotope

13 Ionic bonding is frequently seen between which types of substances?

- [ ] a. A metal and a non-metal
- [ ] b. A metal and a solid non-metal
- [ ] c. Two metals only
- [ ] d. Two non-metal elements

14 What is the name given to the type of bonding involving sharing of electrons?

- [ ] a. Atomic
- [ ] b. Electrovalent
- [ ] c. Ionic
- [ ] d. Covalent

15 Which of the following describes the physical properties of ionic substances?

☐ a. High melting points and low boiling points
☐ b. Low melting points and high boiling points
☐ c. High melting points and conduction of electricity
☐ d. Low melting points and conduction of electricity

16 Which of the following describes the type of bonding in metals?

☐ a. They possess covalent bonds
☐ b. Ionic bonds occur by the sharing of electrons
☐ c. Outer orbits of metal atoms overlap to produce free electrons
☐ d. The inner orbits of electrons overlap to allow the atoms to migrate

17 Sodium has an atomic number of 11. How are the electrons arranged?

☐ a. 2.8.1
☐ b. 2.2.7
☐ c. 8.2.1
☐ d. 8.3

18 Which of the following statements describes graphite?

☐ a. Carbon atoms are arranged in single six-sided rings
☐ b. Carbon atoms are arranged in a tetrahedral lattice
☐ c. Carbon atoms are arranged in layers of hexagons
☐ d. Carbon atoms are arranged in layers of octagons

19 What is the relative molecular mass of sulphuric acid?

☐ a. 136
☐ b. 66
☐ c. 98
☐ d. 49

20 What is the mass of two moles of water?

☐ a. 36 g
☐ b. 18 g
☐ c. 17 g
☐ d. 39 g

Elements, compounds, and mixtures

21 What is an element?

☐ a. A pure substance made of one type of atom
☐ b. A substance in group I of the periodic table
☐ c. A metal
☐ d. A mixture of two atoms

22 Iron from a blast furnace melts at around 1200°C but the melting point of iron is 1500°C. Why is this so?

☐ a. The iron is more pure
☐ b. Adding impurities lowers the melting point
☐ c. The iron melts faster in the furnace
☐ d. The iron has an oxidation agent added

23 Which of the following is a transition metal?

☐ a. Calcium
☐ b. Aluminium

☐ c. Lead
☐ d. Silver

24 Which of the following elements are gases at room temperature and pressure?

☐ a. Carbon and chlorine
☐ b. Argon and chlorine
☐ c. Chlorine and iodine
☐ d. Sulphur and fluorine

25 Which of the following elements is a solid non-metal?

☐ a. Iodine
☐ b. Nitrogen
☐ c. Bromine
☐ d. Nickel

26 Which of the following are alkali metals?

☐ a. Magnesium and francium
☐ b. Sodium and calcium
☐ c. Lithium and boron
☐ d. Potassium and caesium

27 The universe is thought to have started with the 'Big Bang'. What were the first substances formed after the 'explosion'?

☐ a. Oxygen and helium
☐ b. Hydrogen and carbon
☐ c. Hydrogen and helium
☐ d. Zinc and chlorine

28 Just by looking, how would one know that a jar contained immiscible liquids?

☐ a. The liquids would be separate and unmixed
☐ b. The liquids would mix totally if shaken and left for 30 minutes

☐ c. The liquids would be mixed
☐ d. The liquids would only begin to separate after standing for 3 days

29 What is chromatography used for?

☐ a. To separate solutes in a solution
☐ b. To make coloured dyes
☐ c. To make locating agents
☐ d. To separate solvents

30 What do impurities do to the boiling point when they are added to a liquid?

☐ a. Whether they raise or lower the boiling point depends upon the amount added
☐ b. They lower the boiling point
☐ c. They raise the boiling point
☐ d. They make no difference

31 What is allotropy?

☐ a. Different crystalline forms of the same element
☐ b. Forms of carbon only
☐ c. Forms of sulphur only
☐ d. Atoms with different numbers of neutrons

32 Alloys are metals blended with other metals. Which one of the following is **not** an alloy?

☐ a. Bronze
☐ b. Tin
☐ c. Steel
☐ d. Brass

33 Potassium, sodium, and lithium are very reactive metals. Which of the following is **not** true?

☐ a. They form alkaline oxides
☐ b. Oxides form slowly without burning
☐ c. They react with cold water
☐ d. They are soft

34 Sulphur is widely used in industry for the vulcanization of rubber, to produce sulphuric acid, as a fungicide, and in the manufacture of paper. Which of the following is **not** true for sulphur?

☐ a. It forms allotropes
☐ b. It is extracted from the ground in the Frasch process
☐ c. It conducts heat
☐ d. It burns with a blue flame

35 Fluorine, chlorine, bromine, iodine, and astatine are halogens and have common characteristics. Which of the following statements is **not** true for halogens?

☐ a. They show trends in physical state
☐ b. They are reducing agents
☐ c. They show trends in colour
☐ d. They are all diatomic molecules

36 In a laboratory, which of the following would indicate if a colourless, odourless liquid is water?

☐ a. Cobalt chloride paper goes blue
☐ b. It turns anhydrous copper(II) sulphate from white to blue
☐ c. It turns anhydrous copper(II) sulphate from blue to white
☐ d. Limewater goes cloudy

37 If an element reacts with copper by burning with a blue flame, what is the element?

☐ a. Sulphur
☐ b. Copper
☐ c. Magnesium
☐ d. Potassium

38 Sodium (a metal) and phosphorus (a non-metal) both burn in oxygen with a yellow flame, but react differently when dissolved in water. Which of the following statements indicates that the element is phosphorus?

☐ a. It is present in fats and carbohydrates
☐ b. It dissolves to give a strongly alkaline solution (pH 14)
☐ c. It dissolves to give a strongly acidic solution (pH 2)
☐ d. It must never be stored in oil or water

39 Which metal is a good conductor of electricity and, because it oxidizes easily, will not tarnish easily?

☐ a. Gold
☐ b. Iron
☐ c. Mercury
☐ d. Aluminium

40 What is an alloy?

☐ a. A combination of isotopes
☐ b. A combination of metals
☐ c. A combination of two non-metals
☐ d. A combination of allotropes

41 There are differences between a compound of elements and a mixture of elements. Which of the following statements refers to compounds?

☐ a. A chemical reaction is needed to split them into simpler substances

☐ b. They are a mixture of two or more elements

☐ c. They are always formed by the transfer of electrons

☐ d. They always conduct electricity

42 Formulae are written for compounds with the formula of a compound consisting of the symbols of the elements present. What does the formula NaOH stand for?

☐ a. Sulphur oxyhydrate
☐ b. Sodium oxide
☐ c. Sodium oxyhydrate
☐ d. Sodium hydroxide

43 A bee sting can be treated with calamine lotion and a wasp sting can be treated with vinegar. What are these treatments examples of?

☐ a. Neutralization
☐ b. Synthesis
☐ c. Displacement
☐ d. Precipitation

44 A pure substance has a definite melting point and, at a standard atmospheric pressure, a specific boiling point. What effect does the presence of impurities have on these points?

☐ a. It increases both the melting and boiling points

☐ b. It decreases both the melting and boiling points

☐ c. It has no effect

☐ d. It lowers the melting point and increases the boiling point slightly

45 Which of the following is true of a compound as opposed to a mixture?

☐ a. Energy is usually given out or taken in during formation

☐ b. Elements can be easily separated

☐ c. It is always made by the sharing of electrons

☐ d. It has physical properties like the elements in it

46 How would one describe particle vibration in a solid as compared to a liquid or gas?

☐ a. Very fast
☐ b. Very slow
☐ c. The particles do not vibrate
☐ d. The same

47 Diamond and graphite are allotropes of which element?

☐ a. Calcium
☐ b. Oxygen
☐ c. Carbon
☐ d. Silicon

48 Which of the following processes does **not** use up oxygen?

☐ a. Combustion
☐ b. Respiration
☐ c. Photosynthesis
☐ d. Oxidation

49 A substance that is a gas has which of the following?

☐ a. Strong force of attraction between the molecules and a definite shape

☐ b. No force of attraction between the molecules and no definite shape

☐ c. Strong force of attraction between the molecules and no definite shape

☐ d. No force of attraction between the molecules and a definite shape

☐ c. The properties of a compound are different from those of its constituent elements

☐ d. The properties of a compound are the same as those of its constituent elements

50 Which of the following statements applies to diffusion?

☐ a. Occurs very quickly
☐ b. Is only seen in living tissue
☐ c. Needs a concentration gradient and is passive (requires no energy)
☐ d. Needs a concentration gradient and is active (requires energy)

51 Which word best describes a substance that changes from a solid to a gas with no liquid stage?

☐ a. Melting
☐ b. Evaporating
☐ c. Freezing
☐ d. Subliming

52 Which of the following is the reason why hydrochloric acid diffuses more slowly than ammonia?

☐ a. Ammonia is an alkaline gas
☐ b. Hydrochloric acid has a pH of 1
☐ c. Hydrochloric acid is a lighter molecule
☐ d. Ammonia is a lighter molecule

53 Which of the following refers to a compound?

☐ a. A compound always has a relatively low melting point
☐ b. A compound contains a mixture of two or more elements

54 Which of the following methods of separation relies on differences in boiling points of the substances?

☐ a. Distillation
☐ b. Chromatography
☐ c. Evaporation
☐ d. Filtration

55 Which of the following pairs of liquids is immiscible?

☐ a. Ammonium hydroxide and water
☐ b. Hydrochloric acid and water
☐ c. Alcohol and water
☐ d. Oil and water

56 Which of the following tests would identify a gas as hydrogen?

☐ a. Turns limewater cloudy
☐ b. Relights a glowing spill
☐ c. Bleaches damp litmus paper
☐ d. Makes a squeaky pop with a lit spill

57 Which of the following gases is strongly acidic?

☐ a. Ammonia
☐ b. Carbon monoxide
☐ c. Oxygen
☐ d. Sulphur dioxide

58 What colour precipitate is obtained when sodium hydroxide solution is added to copper sulphate solution?

☐ a. White
☐ b. Green
☐ c. Black
☐ d. Blue

59 Which of the following statements is **true** for a two-carbon alcohol?

☐ a. Name: methanol; contains –COOH group
☐ b. Name: methanol; contains –OH group
☐ c. Name: ethanol; contains –OH group
☐ d. Name: ethanol; contains –COOH group

60 Which property of metals means that they can be drawn into wires?

☐ a. Ductile
☐ b. Malleable
☐ c. Conductive
☐ d. Sonorous

61 Which substance is partially removed from iron, leaving around 1%, to make mild steel?

☐ a. Manganese
☐ b. Carbon
☐ c. Nickel
☐ d. Zinc

62 Copper metal is put into silver nitrate solution. After a few minutes a dark solid appears. Which of the following describes what has happened?

☐ a. A displacement reaction occurred; silver formed
☐ b. A decomposition reaction occurred; copper oxide formed

☐ c. A displacement reaction occurred; copper formed
☐ d. A decomposition reaction occurred; copper formed

63 What is the atomic mass expressed in grams known as?

☐ a. The mole
☐ b. The product
☐ c. The mass number
☐ d. The formula

64 Which of the following statements is true about an element in group VII?

☐ a. Non-metal, 7 electrons in the outer shell, valency 1
☐ b. Non-metal, 1 electron in outer shell, valency 7
☐ c. Metal, 7 electrons in outer shell, valency 1
☐ d. Non-metal, 7 electrons in the outer shell, valency 7

65 Which of the following describes metals in group I?

☐ a. Hard, reactive, called alkali metals
☐ b. Hard, reactive, called alkaline earth metals
☐ c. Soft, reactive, called alkaline earth metals
☐ d. Soft, reactive, called alkali metals

66 In which part of the periodic table would one find metals that can act as catalysts?

☐ a. Group I
☐ b. Group II
☐ c. Group III
☐ d. Transition metal group

67 Which element is in the same period as calcium?

☐ a. Lead
☐ b. Potassium
☐ c. Aluminium
☐ d. Magnesium

68 The halogens show a trend in colour and state. Which of the following statements is true?

☐ a. Bromine is an orange liquid; chlorine is a green solid
☐ b. Bromine is an orange liquid; chlorine is a green gas
☐ c. Bromine is an orange solid; chlorine is a green gas
☐ d. Bromine is an orange gas; chlorine is a green gas

69 How does reactivity change down groups in the periodic table?

☐ a. Increases down both metal and non-metal groups
☐ b. Decreases down a metal group and increases down a non-metal group
☐ c. Increases down a metal group and decreases down a non-metal group
☐ d. Decreases down both metal and non-metal groups

70 Which of the following describes why neon is an inert gas?

☐ a. It is a noble gas
☐ b. It is in group VI
☐ c. It has a full outer shell of eight electrons
☐ d. It has a full outer shell of two electrons

71 When chlorine is bubbled into potassium bromide which of the following occurs?

☐ a. Chlorine displaces potassium
☐ b. Potassium chlorate forms
☐ c. Chlorine displaces bromine
☐ d. No reaction

72 When silver nitrate is added to potassium chloride a precipitate is formed. What is the colour of this precipitate?

☐ a. White
☐ b. Blue
☐ c. Black
☐ d. Lilac

73 Which pH number would identify a strong acid?

☐ a. 1
☐ b. 5
☐ c. 9
☐ d. 13

74 Which of the following do all acids contain?

☐ a. Chloride ions
☐ b. Sulphate ions
☐ c. H^+ ions
☐ d. OH^- ions

75 Which of the following statements is true of bases?

☐ a. They all form alkalis
☐ b. They are metal oxides and if soluble form alkalis
☐ c. They are metal carbonates and react with alkalis
☐ d. They are metal oxides and if soluble form acids

76 Where are metalloids found in the periodic table?

- ☐ a. Anywhere in groups I to III
- ☐ b. In the middle
- ☐ c. On the right
- ☐ d. On the far left

77 Which of the following pairs of substances is used to produce oxygen?

- ☐ a. Sodium carbonate and sulphuric acid
- ☐ b. Zinc and hydrochloric acid
- ☐ c. Sodium hypochlorite and hydrochloric acid
- ☐ d. Hydrogen peroxide and manganese(IV) oxide

78 Which of the following is a way of checking the purity of a substance?

- ☐ a. Measure the boiling point
- ☐ b. Check the colour of the substance
- ☐ c. Add acid and test the gas evolved
- ☐ d. Add indicator and check the colour

79 Which of the following will happen if salt is added to water?

- ☐ a. Raise the boiling point and lower the freezing point
- ☐ b. Lower both the freezing point and the boiling point
- ☐ c. Lower the boiling point and raise the freezing point
- ☐ d. Raise both the freezing point and the boiling point

Chemical reactions

80 What is the balanced symbol equation for the formation of methanol?

- ☐ a. $CO(g) + 2H_2(g) = CH_3OH(g)$
- ☐ b. $2C(s) + 4H_2(g) + O_2(g) = 2CH_3OH(g)$
- ☐ c. $CH_3OH = CO(g) + 2H_2(g)$
- ☐ d. $2CO(g) + 3H_2(g) = CH_3CH_2OH(g)$

81 Which is the balanced symbol equation for the reaction of iron oxide with carbon monoxide?

- ☐ a. $2FeO(s) + 2CO_2(g) = 2Fe(l) + 2CO_2(g) + O_2(g)$
- ☐ b. $Fe_2O_3(s) + 3CO(g) = 2Fe(l) + 3CO_2(g)$
- ☐ c. $FeO_2(s) + 2CO(g) = Fe(l) + 2CO_2(g)$
- ☐ d. $FeO(s) + CO(g) = Fe(l) + CO_2(g)$

82 The Haber process is used to make ammonia. What temperature and pressure produce the highest possible yield of ammonia?

- ☐ a. High pressures and low temperatures
- ☐ b. High pressures and high temperatures
- ☐ c. Low pressures and low temperatures
- ☐ d. Low pressures and high temperatures

83 Which of the following conditions is necessary for a reversible reaction to establish 'dynamic equilibrium' in the Haber process?

☐ a. Use of dilution
☐ b. A cooled vessel
☐ c. An open container
☐ d. A closed container

84 Chemical and nuclear reactions that give out energy are exothermic reactions; those that take in energy are endothermic reactions. Which of the following is **not** true for exothermic reactions?

☐ a. They are rarely reversible
☐ b. Thermal dissociation
☐ c. They do not create energy
☐ d. They raise the temperature of the reacting mixture

85 A non-metal forms a Y^{2-} particle. Which of the following describes the chemical process that has occurred?

☐ a. Atomization
☐ b. Reduction
☐ c. Oxidation
☐ d. Neutralization

86 In an equation what symbol is used to represent a solution?

☐ a. (aq)
☐ b. (g)
☐ c. (s)
☐ d. (l)

87 In a reaction between 24 g of magnesium and excess acid, 50 cm³ of hydrogen was made. The reaction was repeated using 24 g of magnesium and more concentrated acid. How much hydrogen would be made this time?

☐ a. It is not possible to tell from the data given
☐ b. 50 cm³
☐ c. More than 50 cm³
☐ d. Less than 50 cm³

88 When a metal is placed in an acid which of the following describes what happens?

☐ a. A reaction never occurs
☐ b. Metals above copper in the reactivity series react to form a salt and hydrogen
☐ c. Metals above copper in the reactivity series react to form a salt and water
☐ d. A reaction always occurs

89 During a titration, acid is added to alkali until the end point is reached. What has happened at this end point?

☐ a. Neutralization
☐ b. Decomposition
☐ c. Precipitation
☐ d. Displacement

90 Which of the following acids can be used to prepare acid salts?

☐ a. Nitric acid
☐ b. Hydrochloric acid
☐ c. Sulphuric acid
☐ d. Acetic acid (ethanoic acid)

91 In order to make copper sulphate, excess copper carbonate is added to sulphuric acid. Why is excess carbonate used?

- ☐ a. To make sure all the mixture remains acidic
- ☐ b. To make sure the copper sulphate is hydrated
- ☐ c. To make sure all the acid is used up
- ☐ d. To make sure a sulphate forms and not a sulphite

92 Which of the following statements about salt solubility is **not** true?

- ☐ a. All potassium salts are insoluble
- ☐ b. Most carbonates are insoluble
- ☐ c. All nitrates are soluble
- ☐ d. All lead salts (except nitrate) are insoluble

93 A zeolite has many tiny holes through it. Why does this make it a good catalyst?

- ☐ a. It allows oxygen in
- ☐ b. It has a large surface area for the reaction to take place
- ☐ c. It has an active site
- ☐ d. It allows air out

94 What effect does an iron catalyst have on the rates of the forward and reverse reactions in the Haber process?

- ☐ a. It slows the forward reaction but speeds up the reverse
- ☐ b. It speeds up the forward and reverse reactions

- ☐ c. It speeds up the forward reaction but slows the reverse
- ☐ d. It slows down both

95 Which of the following is true of a catalyst?

- ☐ a. It is slowly used up during the reaction
- ☐ b. It is always iron
- ☐ c. It alters the position of equilibrium
- ☐ d. It can alter the rate of reaction but remains chemically unchanged at the end of the reaction

96 Which of the following metals is often used as a catalyst?

- ☐ a. Lithium
- ☐ b. Aluminium
- ☐ c. Gold
- ☐ d. Iron

97 Enzymes are biological catalysts. Which statement is **not** true of enzymes?

- ☐ a. Enzymes are protein molecules
- ☐ b. Enzymes are poisoned by heavy metals
- ☐ c. Enzymes are deactivated by heat
- ☐ d. Enzymes are used up during a reaction

98 What is produced by heating wood in the absence of air?

- ☐ a. Carbon monoxide
- ☐ b. Charcoal
- ☐ c. Water
- ☐ d. Diamond

99 What type of reaction is the conversion of methanol to methanoic acid?

☐ a. Oxidation
☐ b. Reduction
☐ c. Decomposition
☐ d. Neutralization

100 During the reaction lead oxide + carbon = lead + carbon dioxide what type of process has taken place?

☐ a. Oxidation
☐ b. Thermite
☐ c. Redox
☐ d. Reduction

101 Which of the following would increase the rate of a reaction?

☐ a. Decreasing the temperature
☐ b. Increasing the concentration of reactants
☐ c. Increasing the volume by adding water
☐ d. Decreasing the pressure

102 Which of the following would decrease the rate of a reaction?

☐ a. Adding a catalyst
☐ b. Decreasing the temperature
☐ c. Increasing the pressure
☐ d. Decreasing the volume

103 In which of the following could the rate of reaction be investigated by collecting the gas given off over set time intervals?

☐ a. Magnesium and oxygen
☐ b. Zinc and hydrochloric acid

☐ c. Hydrochloric acid and sodium hydroxide
☐ d. Potassium iodide and lead nitrate

104 Which statement describes why the rate of reaction can be followed in the reaction between sodium thiosulphate and hydrochloric acid?

☐ a. The mixture gives off hydrogen gas
☐ b. The mixture turns cloudy as sodium is deposited
☐ c. The mixture gives off chlorine gas
☐ d. The mixture turns cloudy as sulphur is deposited

105 The speed of a reaction between magnesium and hydrochloric acid is increased by grinding the magnesium to a fine powder. Which of the following statements explains why this happens?

☐ a. The powder has a larger surface area
☐ b. The powder has a smaller surface area
☐ c. The grinding made the acid warm
☐ d. The grinding made the magnesium atoms vibrate

106 What type of reaction takes place when iron oxide is converted to iron?

☐ a. Oxidation
☐ b. Addition
☐ c. Reduction
☐ d. Substitution

107 Which of the following metals has a protective oxide coating that hides its true reactivity?

☐ a. Iron
☐ b. Zinc
☐ c. Aluminium
☐ d. Copper

108 Which two substances are needed to make iron rust?

☐ a. Hydrogen and water
☐ b. Oxygen and water
☐ c. Carbon dioxide and water
☐ d. Carbon monoxide and water

109 What is the name given to the method of protecting iron by placing a more reactive metal block (usually magnesium or zinc) onto iron?

☐ a. Painting
☐ b. Plating
☐ c. Sacrificial protection
☐ d. Galvanizing

110 Which of the following carbonates decomposes when heated?

☐ a. Calcium carbonate
☐ b. Aluminium carbonate
☐ c. Copper carbonate
☐ d. Sodium carbonate

111 Which metal reacts with nitric acid?

☐ a. Calcium
☐ b. Platinum
☐ c. Copper
☐ d. Gold

112 Which gas is given off when lead nitrate is heated?

☐ a. Nitrogen monoxide
☐ b. Carbon dioxide
☐ c. Nitrogen dioxide
☐ d. Nitrogen

113 In an experiment to copper plate a zinc disc, which arrangement should be used?

☐ a. Anode of copper, cathode of zinc, and copper sulphate solution
☐ b. Anode of copper, cathode of zinc, and zinc sulphate solution
☐ c. Anode of zinc, cathode of copper, and zinc sulphate solution
☐ d. Anode of zinc, cathode of copper, and copper sulphate solution

Changing and using materials

114 Which very soft mineral, used in powdered form in cosmetics, is ranked No. 1 on the Mohs scale of hardness?

☐ a. Magnesite
☐ b. Plaster
☐ c. Talc
☐ d. Haematite

115 Polytetrafluoroethene is a plastic known by its abbreviation PTFE. What is its special quality, useful in the kitchen?

☐ a. It is thermosetting
☐ b. It is non-stick
☐ c. It will decompose
☐ d. It is non-abrasive

116 How is naphtha produced?

☐ a. By fractional distillation of crude oil
☐ b. Via the contact process
☐ c. By precipitation
☐ d. By synthesis

117 What are the two main elements in naphtha?

☐ a. Carbon and nitrogen
☐ b. Carbon and oxygen
☐ c. Oxygen and hydrogen
☐ d. Carbon and hydrogen

118 Naphtha is converted into ethene by a process of cracking. Which of the following conditions is necessary for cracking?

☐ a. Low temperature
☐ b. High temperature
☐ c. Presence of oxygen
☐ d. Low pressure

119 What is polymerization?

☐ a. Breaking long chains to smaller molecules
☐ b. Joining together of short molecules to form long chains
☐ c. Joining two molecules together
☐ d. Removing oxygen

120 What is the difference between alkanes and alkenes?

☐ a. Alkanes are unsaturated and alkenes are saturated
☐ b. Alkanes contain nitrogen
☐ c. Alkenes contain nitrogen
☐ d. Alkanes are saturated and alkenes are unsaturated

121 How could one test a hydrocarbon to see whether it is an alkane or an alkene?

☐ a. Alkanes turn bromine water colourless
☐ b. Alkenes turn bromine water colourless
☐ c. Alkenes are always heavier
☐ d. Alkanes undergo addition reactions

122 What is the process called in which liquid turns to vapour if left standing?

☐ a. Condensation
☐ b. Sublimation
☐ c. Evaporation
☐ d. Transpiration

123 Carboxylic acids react with alcohols to form esters. What are esters used for?

☐ a. As food additives and solvents
☐ b. As fertilizers
☐ c. As petrol substitutes
☐ d. As substitute protein

124 Drugs are chemical substances given to relieve the body of disease or symptoms of disease. Which of the following drugs would be given to relieve pain?

☐ a. Sedatives
☐ b. Analgesics
☐ c. Antiseptics
☐ d. Stimulants

125 Making polythene from ethene is an example of what?

☐ a. Cracking
☐ b. Substitution polymerization

c. Formation of an ester bond

d. Addition polymerization

126 Which of the following is the term used to describe the breaking of large organic molecules into smaller ones?

a. Hydrogenation

b. Breaking

c. Catalytic oxidation

d. Cracking

127 In what order would the following substances be obtained during the distillation of crude oil (starting with the heaviest substance)?

a. Bitumen, petrol, diesel, gas

b. Bitumen, diesel, petrol, gas

c. Diesel, petrol, bitumen, gas

d. Diesel, bitumen, petrol, gas

128 Which two substances are always made when a hydrocarbon is burned in a limited oxygen supply?

a. Carbon monoxide and nitrogen

b. Hydrogen and water

c. Carbon dioxide and hydrogen

d. Water and carbon monoxide

129 An unsaturated fat would contain which of the following?

a. Carbon to carbon double bonds

b. Carbon to carbon single bonds

c. Carbon to oxygen double bonds

d. Carbon to hydrogen double bonds

130 Some organic molecules react by opening up double bonds to form new compounds. What is the name given to this chemical process?

a. Cracking

b. Addition

c. Substitution

d. Combustion

131 Monomers are joined together to make polymers. Which of the following pairs is the correct polymer and monomer?

a. Ethene and polystyrene

b. Ethane and polythene

c. Propene and polythene

d. Ethene and polythene

132 Which of the following metals can be extracted from its ore by heating with carbon?

a. Lead

b. Aluminium

c. Magnesium

d. Lithium

133 Which of the following is the form of iron ore added to a blast furnace?

a. Magnesite

b. Malachite

c. Haematite

d. Bauxite

134 In a blast furnace which substance acts as the reducing agent?

a. Carbon monoxide

b. Hydrogen

c. Limestone

d. Carbon dioxide

135 In a blast furnace which substance is added to the charge to remove impurities?

☐ a. Limestone
☐ b. Lime
☐ c. Coke
☐ d. Slag

136 In the production of aluminium the oxide ore is first dissolved in another molten ore of aluminium. What is the name of this molten ore?

☐ a. Anodite
☐ b. Fluorite
☐ c. Cryolite
☐ d. Kryptonite

137 In electrolysis of molten sodium chloride which of the following occurs?

☐ a. Sodium forms at the cathode
☐ b. Sodium forms at the anode
☐ c. Hydrogen forms at the cathode
☐ d. Hydrogen forms at the anode

138 In the electrolysis of aqueous sodium chloride which of the following occurs?

☐ a. Sodium forms at the cathode
☐ b. Hydrogen forms at the anode
☐ c. Sodium forms at the anode
☐ d. Hydrogen forms at the cathode

139 In the electrolysis of copper sulphate solution which substance is formed at the anode?

☐ a. Copper
☐ b. Oxygen
☐ c. Sulphur
☐ d. Hydrogen

140 Which type of organism turns gaseous nitrogen in the air into nitrate compounds in the soil, as shown in the nitrogen cycle?

☐ a. Denitrifying bacteria
☐ b. Viruses
☐ c. Nitrifying bacteria
☐ d. Nitrogen-fixing bacteria

141 Which of the following is an example of a physical change?

☐ a. Wood burning
☐ b. Oxidizing iron (2+) ions to iron metal
☐ c. Iodine crystals subliming to iodine vapour
☐ d. Reacting zinc in hydrochloric acid

142 Which of the following is an example of a chemical change?

☐ a. Distilling alcohol from an alcohol and water mixture
☐ b. Melting naphtha
☐ c. Mixing iron and sulphur
☐ d. Adding lithium to water

143 Which of the following is **not** an example of a reversible change?

☐ a. Heating hydrated copper sulphate
☐ b. Reacting magnesium in oxygen gas
☐ c. Reacting nitrogen and hydrogen to form ammonia
☐ d. Reacting sulphur dioxide with oxygen to form sulphur trioxide

144 Which of the following is a use of sulphur dioxide?

☐ a. Indicator
☐ b. Fertilizer
☐ c. Fuel
☐ d. Food preservative

Earth and air

145 Which type of rock crystallizes on the surface when liquid magma reaches the Earth's surface?

☐ a. Metamorphic
☐ b. Sedimentary
☐ c. Intrusive igneous
☐ d. Extrusive igneous

146 Which type of rock are fossils found in?

☐ a. Extrusive igneous
☐ b. Sedimentary
☐ c. Metamorphic
☐ d. Intrusive igneous

147 What is the result when two plates in the Earth's crust collide head on?

☐ a. A mountain range
☐ b. An earthquake
☐ c. An oceanic trench
☐ d. A volcano

148 Which of the following statements about the Earth's structure is **true**?

☐ a. The outer core is liquid iron and nickel
☐ b. The mantle is solid rock
☐ c. The crust is solid and thick (100 km)

☐ d. The inner core is liquid iron and nickel

149 Which of the following pollutants is the main cause of acid rain?

☐ a. Sulphur dioxide
☐ b. Carbon monoxide
☐ c. Lead vapour
☐ d. Carbon dioxide

150 In the water cycle, water vapour can enter the atmosphere via its loss through the leaves of plants. What is this process called?

☐ a. Percolation
☐ b. Evaporation
☐ c. Transpiration
☐ d. Condensation

Physics Questions

1 Which instrument measures electric current?

☐ a. Wattmeter
☐ b. Ammeter
☐ c. Ampmeter
☐ d. Voltmeter

2 Which of the following is a good conductor of electricity?

☐ a. Polythene
☐ b. Rubber
☐ c. Copper
☐ d. Plastic

3 If electricity costs 10p per kilowatt-hour, how much would it cost to operate a 3-kilowatt fire for 2 hours?

☐ a. 20p
☐ b. 0.6p
☐ c. 60p
☐ d. 600p

4 What term is used to show the amount of energy given to each coulomb of charge as it passes through a battery?

☐ a. Resistance
☐ b. Power
☐ c. Voltage
☐ d. Amps

5 A diode is a rectifier. This means that it allows current to flow in which direction?

☐ a. In only one direction
☐ b. In both directions
☐ c. In neither direction
☐ d. In the opposite direction

6 A diode is made of what type of material?

☐ a. Aluminium
☐ b. Plastic
☐ c. Copper
☐ d. Semiconductor

7 What part of an atom is negatively charged?

☐ a. Proton
☐ b. Neutron
☐ c. Electron
☐ d. Nucleus

8 If an object has become positively charged, what is most likely to have happened?

☐ a. It has gained electrons
☐ b. It has lost protons

☐ c. It has lost electrons
☐ d. It has gained energy

9 What is an ion?

☐ a. A molecule
☐ b. A compound
☐ c. An atom or group of atoms with a charge
☐ d. An uncharged atom

10 Electric current is a flow of which particle?

☐ a. Protons
☐ b. Atoms
☐ c. Neutrons
☐ d. Electrons

11 When using Fleming's left-hand rule, what does the position of the thumb show?

☐ a. The size of the force
☐ b. Direction of the force
☐ c. Direction of the current
☐ d. Direction of the magnetic field

12 Why does a double insulated hairdryer have no earth wire connected to it?

☐ a. It has a fuse
☐ b. Its outer casing is made of plastic
☐ c. The wires inside have two layers of plastic
☐ d. It has no live wire

13 If a bar magnet is pushed into a solenoid, how can the induced voltage (and current) be increased?

☐ a. Moving the magnet faster
☐ b. Moving the magnet slower

☐ c. Using a soft iron bar instead of a magnet
☐ d. Decreasing the number of turns on the coil

14 Which material is used to make an electromagnet?

☐ a. Aluminium
☐ b. Brass
☐ c. Steel
☐ d. Iron

15 The strength of an electromagnet can be increased in a number of ways. Which of the following will not have this effect?

☐ a. Using more current
☐ b. Using more turns of wire on the core
☐ c. Using a copper core
☐ d. Bringing the poles closer together

16 In which of the following is an electromagnet not used?

☐ a. Electric bells
☐ b. Telephone earpieces
☐ c. Batteries
☐ d. Relays

17 Which of the following statements on magnets is not true?

☐ a. The north poles attract each other
☐ b. Opposite poles attract each other
☐ c. A magnet has a north and a south pole
☐ d. Magnets have two poles

18 What is the region around a magnet called?

☐ a. Polar field
☐ b. Electric field
☐ c. An electromagnet
☐ d. Magnetic field

19 What is the frequency in hertz (Hz) of the electricity supply to a normal house?

☐ a. 240 Hz
☐ b. 50 Hz
☐ c. 3 Hz
☐ d. 120 Hz

20 Which of these calculations correctly uses Ohm's law to calculate the resistance of a component?

☐ a. Current divided by voltage
☐ b. Voltage divided by current
☐ c. Current multiplied by voltage
☐ d. Voltage multiplied by current

21 What is the resistance of a lamp, when the voltage across it is 10 volts, and the current in the circuit is 2 amps?

☐ a. 0.5 ohms
☐ b. 10 ohms
☐ c. 5 ohms
☐ d. 20 ohms

22 What colour is the earth wire of a three-pin plug?

☐ a. Green and yellow
☐ b. Red
☐ c. Brown
☐ d. Blue

23 Which wire is connected to the fuse in a three-pin plug?

☐ a. Brown
☐ b. Black
☐ c. Green and yellow
☐ d. Blue

24 An appliance has a potential difference of 24 volts across it and a current of 3 amps through it. Calculate its power in watts (W).

☐ a. 21 W
☐ b. 27 W
☐ c. 8 W
☐ d. 72 W

25 Which of the following does not affect the resistance of a wire?

☐ a. The thickness of the wire
☐ b. The length of the wire
☐ c. The components connected to the wire
☐ d. The temperature of the wire

26 Calculate the combined resistance of two resistors (of 4 ohms and 8 ohms) connected in series.

☐ a. 32 ohms
☐ b. 4 ohms
☐ c. 2 ohms
☐ d. 12 ohms

27 What would happen to a bulb if the resistance of a variable resistor is reduced?

☐ a. There is no change
☐ b. The bulb gets dimmer
☐ c. The bulb gets brighter
☐ d. The bulb goes out

28 Two resistors (of 3 ohms and 6 ohms) are connected in parallel. Calculate the combined resistance.

☐ a. 2 ohms
☐ b. 9 ohms
☐ c. 18 ohms
☐ d. 0.5 ohms

29 Which of the following fuses would be most suitable to use when an appliance of 3 kilowatts is connected to a 240-volt supply?

☐ a. 5 A
☐ b. 30 A
☐ c. 10 A
☐ d. 15 A

30 If polythene is rubbed with a dry cloth what will happen?

☐ a. It becomes positively charged
☐ b. Its charge stays the same
☐ c. It removes the charge
☐ d. It becomes negatively charged

31 When two polythene strips which have been rubbed with a woollen cloth are brought together they repel each other. Why is this?

☐ a. They are both positively charged
☐ b. Both are uncharged
☐ c. One is positively charged, one is negatively charged
☐ d. They are both negatively charged

32 What is the unit of static charge?

☐ a. Watt
☐ b. Coulomb
☐ c. Ohm
☐ d. Volt

33 What effect would a step-down transformer have on voltage?

☐ a. Slightly increase it
☐ b. There would be no change
☐ c. Greatly increase it
☐ d. Decrease it

34 A step-down transformer has 200 turns on the primary coil with a voltage of 240 volts. If the secondary coil has 50 turns, what will the output voltage (V) be?

☐ a. 120 V
☐ b. 60 V
☐ c. 50 V
☐ d. 960 V

35 The primary coil of a transformer has 10 turns and the secondary coil has 100 turns. If the input voltage is 20 V, what is the output voltage?

☐ a. 5 V
☐ b. 2 V
☐ c. 2000 V
☐ d. 200 V

Forces and motion

36 If the space shuttle has a mass of 150,000 kg and the rockets produce a force of 30,000 newtons (N), what acceleration is produced?

☐ a. 45 m/s^2
☐ b. 5 m/s^2
☐ c. 0.2 m/s^2
☐ d. 3 m/s^2

37 A woman jumps from a plane, freefalls for 1,000 m and then opens her parachute. The parachute has the effect of slowing her down. What is the reason for this?

☐ a. The friction created by the parachute exerts a downward force
☐ b. The parachute increases the effect of gravity
☐ c. The extra air resistance created by the parachute slows her down
☐ d. The parachute increases the weight of the person

38 If two forces are acting on an object, what is the overall force acting on it called?

☐ a. Resultant force
☐ b. Combined force
☐ c. Scalar force
☐ d. Frictional force

39 Which of the following quantities has the same units as weight?

☐ a. Power
☐ b. Mass
☐ c. Force
☐ d. Work

40 A mass has a reluctance to change its motion. What is this called?

☐ a. Momentum
☐ b. Inertia
☐ c. Weight
☐ d. Velocity

41 What is the turning effect of a force of 15 newtons (N) acting on a spanner of length 10 cm?

☐ a. 0.15 newton metres (Nm)
☐ b. 150 Nm
☐ c. 1.5 Nm
☐ d. 15 Nm

42 A car is travelling north. What is the direction of the frictional force acting on it?

☐ a. South
☐ b. North
☐ c. East
☐ d. West

43 A book is being pushed along a table. Which of the following statements is true?

☐ a. Neither object incurs a frictional force
☐ b. Only the book incurs a frictional force
☐ c. Only the table incurs a frictional force
☐ d. Both objects incur a frictional force

44 If a gas is compressed until its volume has halved, what happens to its pressure?

☐ a. It is one quarter as great
☐ b. It is four times as great
☐ c. It is twice as great
☐ d. It is half as great

45 If an object has a weight on Earth of 150 newtons (N), what is its mass?

☐ a. 15 kg
☐ b. 1,500 kg
☐ c. 1.5 kg
☐ d. 150 N

46 How would your mass and weight be affected by being on Jupiter?

☐ a. Mass the same, weight greater
☐ b. Mass and weight less
☐ c. Mass and weight stay the same
☐ d. Mass and weight greater

47 A stone is dropped from a tall building. The moment that it leaves the person's hand it will be what?

☐ a. Moving at a constant speed
☐ b. Accelerating
☐ c. Decelerating
☐ d. Moving at a constant velocity

48 Which of the following correctly describes Hooke's law?

☐ a. Extension is directly proportional to the load
☐ b. Extension is inversely proportional to the load
☐ c. Extension is not directly proportional to the load
☐ d. Extension is indirectly proportional to the load

49 If a force of 100 newtons (N) is applied to a spring, its length increases from 10 cm to 30 cm. If this force is replaced by one of 50 N, what is the length of the spring?

☐ a. 20 cm
☐ b. 15 cm
☐ c. 40 cm
☐ d. 25 cm

50 What is the most important quality of the liquid in a hydraulic system?

☐ a. It has a high density
☐ b. It has a low boiling point
☐ c. It can easily be compressed
☐ d. It is not easily compressed

51 A stone is thrown into the air at 30 m per second (m/s). Calculate how high it goes (gravity=10 m/s^2)

☐ a. 600 m
☐ b. 60 m
☐ c. 76 m
☐ d. 45 m

52 When a mass has no resultant force on it, if it is at rest it stays at rest and if it is moving it keeps moving at a constant speed in a straight line. This is an explanation of which law?

☐ a. Newton's third law
☐ b. Newton's first law
☐ c. Hooke's law
☐ d. Snell's law

53 What is the unit of measurement of pressure?

☐ a. Watt
☐ b. Pascal
☐ c. Joule
☐ d. Newton

54 The calculation for pressure can be shown by which of the following equations?

☐ a. Force × area
☐ b. Area ÷ force
☐ c. Area × force
☐ d. Force ÷ area

55 Snowshoes work for which of the following reasons?

☐ a. The pressure is higher because of the large surface area of the shoe

☐ b. The pressure is lower because of the large surface area of the shoe

☐ c. The pressure is higher because of the small surface area of the shoe

☐ d. The pressure is lower because of the small surface area of the shoe

56 Dams are used to control the rate of water flow and to produce hydroelectric power. The wall of a dam is thicker at the bottom than at the top. What is the reason for this?

☐ a. Pressure decreases as depth increases

☐ b. There is a larger volume of water in contact with the dam at the bottom

☐ c. The pressure of the water is higher at greater depths

☐ d. The pressure of the water is greater near the top of the dam

57 A car travels 400 m in 20 seconds. What is its average speed?

☐ a. 20 m/s
☐ b. 10 m/s
☐ c. 420 m/s
☐ d. 8,000 m/s

58 Which of the following will not affect the stopping distance of a car?

☐ a. Road conditions
☐ b. The car's velocity
☐ c. Driver airbags
☐ d. The reaction time of the driver

59 Why are icy roads dangerous?

☐ a. The ice reduces friction, making stopping easier

☐ b. The ice reduces friction, making stopping harder

☐ c. The ice increases friction, making stopping harder

☐ d. The ice reduces the braking distance

60 An object falling from the sky will reach terminal velocity. This is due to what?

☐ a. The object's velocity is increasing

☐ b. The object's acceleration is constant

☐ c. The object's mass is constant

☐ d. The downward force due to gravity is equal to the upward force of the air resistance

61 A car starts from rest and accelerates at 4 m per second (m/s) for 5 seconds. Calculate its final velocity.

☐ a. 20 m/s
☐ b. 1.25 m/s
☐ c. 0.8 m/s
☐ d. 80 m/s

Waves

62 If the volume of a Walkman is increased, this will result in an increase in what?

☐ a. Frequency
☐ b. Pitch
☐ c. Amplitude
☐ d. Wavelength

63 If straight water waves are passed through a narrow gap in a barrier, the waves spread out after passing through the gap. What is the name of this effect?

☐ **a.** Dispersion
☐ **b.** Refraction
☐ **c.** Reflection
☐ **d.** Diffraction

64 A house situated near hills will have better reception for radio signals than for television. Why is this?

☐ **a.** Television waves have a longer wavelength
☐ **b.** Radio waves are refracted
☐ **c.** Radio waves are diffracted more
☐ **d.** Radio waves are diffracted less

65 Which of the following parts of the electromagnetic spectrum has the longest wavelength?

☐ **a.** Infrared
☐ **b.** Radio
☐ **c.** Gamma rays
☐ **d.** Ultraviolet

66 Which part of the electromagnetic spectrum is used to cook your food in a gas oven?

☐ **a.** Infrared
☐ **b.** Radio waves
☐ **c.** Ultraviolet
☐ **d.** Gamma rays

67 What is the unit of frequency of a wave?

☐ **a.** Amplitude
☐ **b.** Metre
☐ **c.** Joule
☐ **d.** Hertz

68 What is the range of hearing for a child?

☐ **a.** 20 Hz–20,000 Hz
☐ **b.** 10 Hz–10,000 Hz
☐ **c.** 5 Hz–50,000 Hz
☐ **d.** 30 Hz–30,000 Hz

69 Which of the following will not increase the natural (resonant) frequency of the string on a guitar?

☐ **a.** Using a lighter string
☐ **b.** Increasing the length
☐ **c.** Shortening the length
☐ **d.** Increasing the tension

70 Which of the following waves is a longitudinal wave?

☐ **a.** Ultraviolet
☐ **b.** Sound
☐ **c.** Microwave
☐ **d.** X-ray

71 An optical fibre is a way in which light can follow a curved path. It can do this due to what?

☐ **a.** Refraction
☐ **b.** Diffraction
☐ **c.** Total internal reflection
☐ **d.** Dispersion

72 Rays of light travelling from air into glass are bent or refracted towards the normal. This is due to what?

☐ **a.** Light travels faster in glass
☐ **b.** The frequency is increased
☐ **c.** Light travels more slowly in glass
☐ **d.** The frequency is decreased

73 A pin is observed through a magnifying glass. Which of the following correctly describes the image of the pin that is seen?

- ☐ a. Inverted, magnified, and real
- ☐ b. Upright, magnified, and virtual
- ☐ c. Upright, magnified, and real
- ☐ d. Upright, diminished, and real

74 What is the calculation for the refractive index of a substance?

- ☐ a. Speed of light in air ÷ speed of light in substance
- ☐ b. Speed of light in water ÷ speed of light in substance
- ☐ c. Speed of light in a vacuum ÷ speed of light in substance
- ☐ d. Speed of light in substance ÷ speed of light in air

75 Which of the following correctly describes seismic waves?

- ☐ a. S-waves are longitudinal, P-waves are longitudinal
- ☐ b. S-waves are transverse, P-waves are transverse
- ☐ c. S-waves are transverse, P-waves are longitudinal
- ☐ d. S-waves are longitudinal, P-waves are transverse

76 If a gun is fired by a man 400 m away, in what order will the sound and light waves reach you?

- ☐ a. They do not reach you
- ☐ b. They arrive together
- ☐ c. Light first, then sound
- ☐ d. Sound first, then light

77 Which of the following does not apply to sound waves?

- ☐ a. They are caused by vibrations
- ☐ b. They can travel through a vacuum
- ☐ c. They travel faster through a solid than a gas
- ☐ d. They are composed of compressions and rarefactions

78 Ultrasound has many applications such as echo-sounding (sonar) on ships. Which of the following best describes the waves?

- ☐ a. High frequency and long wavelength
- ☐ b. Low frequency and long wavelength
- ☐ c. Low frequency and short wavelength
- ☐ d. High frequency and short wavelength

79 Which of the following is the correct calculation to find the speed of a wave?

- ☐ a. Frequency × amplitude
- ☐ b. Frequency × wavelength
- ☐ c. Frequency ÷ wavelength
- ☐ d. Wavelength ÷ frequency

80 Calculate the speed of a wave that has a frequency of 2 hertz (Hz) and a wavelength of 20 cm.

- ☐ a. 40 cm/s
- ☐ b. 22 cm/s
- ☐ c. 10 cm/s
- ☐ d. 18 cm/s

81 If the speed of sound in water is 1,500 m per second (m/s), what would be the wavelength of an audible sound of 1,500 hertz (Hz)?

☐ a. 1,500 m
☐ b. 1.5 m
☐ c. 15 m
☐ d. 1 m

82 If the speed of sound in air is taken as 300 m per second (m/s), how far away is a storm if the thunder is heard 10 seconds after the lightning?

☐ a. 3 km
☐ b. 3,000 km
☐ c. 0.03 km
☐ d. 30 km

The Earth and beyond

83 The asteroid belt is a part of the Solar System where large pieces of rock are in orbit around the Sun. Between which two planets is it situated?

☐ a. Mars and Jupiter
☐ b. Saturn and Uranus
☐ c. Earth and Mars
☐ d. Jupiter and Saturn

84 A comet is a lump of rock and ice that orbits the Sun. During which part of its orbit would it have the highest velocity?

☐ a. As it leaves the Solar System
☐ b. As it enters the Solar System
☐ c. As it passes the Earth
☐ d. When it is closest to the Sun

85 What is a day?

☐ a. The time taken for the Earth to rotate once on its axis
☐ b. The time taken for the Earth to orbit the Sun
☐ c. The time taken for the Earth to orbit the Moon
☐ d. The time taken for the Moon to orbit the Earth

86 What is a year?

☐ a. The time taken for the Earth to rotate on its axis
☐ b. The time taken for the Earth to orbit the Sun
☐ c. The time taken for the Sun to orbit the Earth
☐ d. The time taken for the moon to orbit the Earth

87 How long does it take for the Earth to make one rotation on its axis?

☐ a. 1 month
☐ b. 1 year
☐ c. 24 hours
☐ d. 12 hours

88 How long does it take for the Earth to orbit the Sun?

☐ a. 24 hours
☐ b. 1 day
☐ c. 1 month
☐ d. $365\frac{1}{4}$ days

89 If it is spring in the northern hemisphere, what season is it in the southern hemisphere?

☐ a. Summer
☐ b. Winter
☐ c. Spring
☐ d. Autumn

90 We get the seasons of the year because the Earth is tilted on its axis. At what angle is it tilted?

☐ a. 25°
☐ b. 23.5°
☐ c. 16.5°
☐ d. 45°

91 Which of the following has the greatest effect on the tides on Earth?

☐ a. The planets
☐ b. The weather
☐ c. The Sun
☐ d. The Moon

92 Which of the following explains a total eclipse of the moon?

☐ a. The Sun travels between the Earth and the Moon
☐ b. The Earth travels between the Moon and the Sun
☐ c. The Moon travels between the Earth and the Sun
☐ d. The Moon travels in front of the Sun

93 Which of the following planets is furthest from the Sun?

☐ a. Venus
☐ b. Jupiter
☐ c. Saturn
☐ d. Earth

94 Which of the following planets has the longest year?

☐ a. Mercury
☐ b. Neptune
☐ c. Saturn
☐ d. Mars

95 Which of the following planets has the highest average temperature?

☐ a. Venus
☐ b. Pluto
☐ c. Mars
☐ d. Earth

96 Which of the following is a satellite of the Earth?

☐ a. Comets
☐ b. The Moon
☐ c. The Sun
☐ d. Mars

97 What is the name given to fixed patterns of stars in the night sky?

☐ a. Asteroids
☐ b. Constellations
☐ c. Galaxies
☐ d. Meteors

98 What is the name given to a collection of 100 million stars?

☐ a. Galaxy
☐ b. Constellation
☐ c. Solar System
☐ d. Universe

99 The Sun is mostly composed of which two elements?

☐ a. Hydrogen and helium
☐ b. Hydrogen and oxygen
☐ c. Hydrogen and uranium
☐ d. Helium and oxygen

100 When the Sun reaches the end of its life, what will it become?

☐ a. A red giant, then a white dwarf
☐ b. A white dwarf, then a red giant
☐ c. A red giant, then a black hole
☐ d. A neutron star, then a red giant

101 What is the name of the process occurring in the Sun?

☐ a. Combustion
☐ b. Oxidation
☐ c. Nuclear fusion
☐ d. Nuclear fission

102 Light from other galaxies that are moving away from us has a red shift. This is an example of what?

☐ a. A singularity
☐ b. Spectrum theory
☐ c. The galaxy effect
☐ d. The Doppler effect

103 The Big Bang theory is used to explain the development of the Universe. What is its most important idea?

☐ a. The nuclear reactions in the stars caused the Universe to develop
☐ b. The Universe is constantly expanding and contracting
☐ c. The Universe was created in a huge explosion
☐ d. The Universe will end in a huge explosion

Work, energy, and power

104 Which of the following is a good conductor of heat?

☐ a. Plastic
☐ b. Glass
☐ c. Aluminium
☐ d. Air

105 A convection current can occur in which of the following?

☐ a. Copper
☐ b. Water
☐ c. Plastic
☐ d. Iron

106 Which of the following show the correct calculation for energy efficiency?

☐ a. Useful energy output/total energy input
☐ b. Total energy input/useful energy output
☐ c. Useful energy input/total energy output
☐ d. Total energy output/useful energy input

107 An electric motor does 40 J of useful work when the total energy input is 80 J. Calculate the efficiency of the motor.

☐ a. 2.0 (200%)
☐ b. 0.4 (40%)
☐ c. 1.0 (100%)
☐ d. 0.5 (50%)

108 An electric fire transfers electrical energy to useful heat energy and is 50% efficient. Some of the energy will be wasted as what?

☐ a. Chemical energy
☐ b. Gravitational energy
☐ c. Light energy
☐ d. Strain energy

109 A man drops a ball from a building from a height of 100 m. Calculate the speed that the ball hits the ground.

- ☐ a. 44.7 m/s
- ☐ b. 49.8 m/s
- ☐ c. 100 m/s
- ☐ d. 34.6 m/s

110 Which of the following is not a fossil fuel?

- ☐ a. Gas
- ☐ b. Oil
- ☐ c. Uranium
- ☐ d. Coal

111 Which two gases are produced when fossil fuels are burned?

- ☐ a. Carbon dioxide and water
- ☐ b. Water and oxygen
- ☐ c. Carbon dioxide and nitrogen
- ☐ d. Oxygen and carbon dioxide

112 Burning coal may also produce sulphur dioxide gas. Why is this bad for the environment?

- ☐ a. It causes the greenhouse effect
- ☐ b. It increases levels of acid rain
- ☐ c. It damages the ozone layer
- ☐ d. It causes El Niño

113 If the mass of a book is 2 kg, what force in newtons (N) will it exert on a table?

- ☐ a. 2 N
- ☐ b. 200 N
- ☐ c. 0.2 N
- ☐ d. 20 N

114 Double-glazed windows are put into houses to improve insulation. Which of the following explains how this is achieved?

- ☐ a. The air trapped between the glass prevents heat leaving by convection
- ☐ b. The glass increases the conduction of heat through the window
- ☐ c. A layer of air is trapped between the glass which is a poor conductor of heat
- ☐ d. The double layer of glass prevents heat leaving by radiation

115 Why does wearing a string vest help to keep you warmer on a cold day?

- ☐ a. A layer of warm, insulating air is trapped next to the skin
- ☐ b. It stops convection currents occurring next to the skin
- ☐ c. It increases the convection currents next to the skin
- ☐ d. It reduces the amount of heat lost by radiation

116 Which of the following is the calculation for kinetic energy?

- ☐ a. $\frac{1}{2} \times$ mass $\times$ speed
- ☐ b. $\frac{1}{2} \times$ weight $\times$ speed^2
- ☐ c. $\frac{1}{2} \times$ mass $\times$ speed^2
- ☐ d. Mass $\times$ speed^2

117 What is the kinetic energy of a car of mass 1,500 kg travelling at 10 m per second (m/s)?

- ☐ a. 7,500 J
- ☐ b. 25,000 J
- ☐ c. 75,000 J
- ☐ d. 15,000 J

118 What is the unit of power?

- ☐ a. Joule
- ☐ b. Watt
- ☐ c. Pascal
- ☐ d. Newton

119 What is the calculation for power?

- ☐ a. Work × time
- ☐ b. Force × distance
- ☐ c. Work ÷ time
- ☐ d. Force ÷ time

120 If 200 joules of energy are used in 20 seconds, how much power is developed?

- ☐ a. 4,000 W
- ☐ b. 0.1 W
- ☐ c. 100 W
- ☐ d. 10 W

121 A boy weighing 400 newtons (N) climbs stairs to a height of 20 m in 10 seconds. How much power has he developed?

- ☐ a. 2 W
- ☐ b. 80,000 W
- ☐ c. 800 W
- ☐ d. 200 W

122 A car of mass 1,000 kg climbs 100 m up a hill in 10 seconds. How much power has it developed?

- ☐ a. 100 kW
- ☐ b. 10,000 W
- ☐ c. 10 kW
- ☐ d. 100 W

123 Four boxes of mass 13 kg are lifted onto a shelf 150 cm high in 3 minutes. Calculate the power developed.

- ☐ a. 10.8 W
- ☐ b. 2600 W
- ☐ c. 4.3 W
- ☐ d. 650 W

124 Which of the following would lose energy the fastest by radiation of heat?

- ☐ a. A dull white surface
- ☐ b. A bright shiny surface
- ☐ c. A shiny blue surface
- ☐ d. A dull black surface

125 Which of the following is the best absorber of heat radiation?

- ☐ a. A shiny black surface
- ☐ b. A dull green surface
- ☐ c. A bright shiny surface
- ☐ d. A dull black surface

126 Solar panels absorb the Sun's radiation and this energy can be used to provide hot water. Which colour would be the most suitable to use on the panel?

- ☐ a. Black
- ☐ b. Red
- ☐ c. White
- ☐ d. Blue

127 Heat energy produced in the fusion reactions in the Sun must travel through the vacuum of space to reach the Earth. By what method does it do this?

- ☐ a. Conduction
- ☐ b. Convection
- ☐ c. Insulation
- ☐ d. Radiation

128 Which of the following calculations is used to calculate work done?

- ☐ a. Energy × force
- ☐ b. Force ÷ distance
- ☐ c. Energy × distance
- ☐ d. Force × distance

129 What is the unit of energy?

- ☐ a. Joule
- ☐ b. Newton
- ☐ c. Torque
- ☐ d. Watt

130 A 20-newton (N) bag is lifted 2 m onto a shelf. How much work has been done?

- ☐ a. 400 J
- ☐ b. 40 N
- ☐ c. 10 J
- ☐ d. 40 J

131 If a girl lifts a box of mass 3 kg onto a shelf 3 m high, how much work is done?

- ☐ a. 10 J
- ☐ b. 9 J
- ☐ c. 1 J
- ☐ d. 90 J

132 An electric appliance has a power rating of 1.5 kW. How many joules of energy are converted in 5 seconds?

- ☐ a. 7.5 J
- ☐ b. 300 J
- ☐ c. 7,500 J
- ☐ d. 0.3 J

Radioactivity

133 What is alpha radiation composed of?

- ☐ a. An electromagnetic wave
- ☐ b. High-energy protons
- ☐ c. Helium nuclei
- ☐ d. High-energy electrons

134 Radium-226 is radioactive. When it decays its mass number decreases to 222 and its atomic number decreases from 88 to 86. What type of particle is emitted?

- ☐ a. Alpha
- ☐ b. Neutron
- ☐ c. Beta
- ☐ d. Proton

135 What is beta radiation composed of?

- ☐ a. An electromagnetic wave
- ☐ b. Helium nuclei
- ☐ c. High-energy electrons
- ☐ d. High-energy neutrons

136 Which of the following best describes the penetration of beta particles?

- ☐ a. Stopped by 1 mm of copper
- ☐ b. Stopped by 3 mm of paper
- ☐ c. Stopped by 6 cm of air
- ☐ d. Stopped by 3 mm of aluminium

137 Polonium-218 has an atomic number of 84 and can decay by beta emission. What will the atomic number be after this emission?

- ☐ a. 85
- ☐ b. 83
- ☐ c. 82
- ☐ d. 84

138 Which of the following is not a method of detecting radioactivity?

- ☐ a. Cloud chamber
- ☐ b. Geiger-Muller tube
- ☐ c. Oscilloscope
- ☐ d. Photographic film

139 What is gamma radiation composed of?

- ☐ a. Helium nuclei
- ☐ b. High-energy electrons
- ☐ c. High-energy neutrons
- ☐ d. A high-energy electromagnetic wave

140 Which type of radiation travels at the speed of light?

- ☐ a. Gamma
- ☐ b. Beta
- ☐ c. Alpha
- ☐ d. All of them

141 What is meant by the term half-life?

- ☐ a. The time it takes for the number of atoms to increase by half
- ☐ b. The time it takes for the number of atoms to reduce by half
- ☐ c. The time it takes for the mass to increase by half
- ☐ d. The time it takes for the mass to reduce by half

142 If a substance has a half-life of 20 years, how much of the original sample will be left after 40 years?

- ☐ a. $\frac{1}{4}$
- ☐ b. $\frac{1}{8}$
- ☐ c. $\frac{1}{2}$
- ☐ d. $\frac{3}{4}$

143 Which of the three types of radiation causes the greatest ionization?

- ☐ a. Gamma
- ☐ b. They all cause equal amounts of ionization
- ☐ c. Alpha
- ☐ d. Beta

144 Most carbon atoms have 6 neutrons, but some have 8 neutrons. They have the same chemical properties but different masses. The name for these different atoms are?

- ☐ a. Nuclei
- ☐ b. Isotopes
- ☐ c. Allotropes
- ☐ d. Molecules

145 Which of the following types of radiation are not affected by electric and magnetic fields?

- ☐ a. Gamma
- ☐ b. Alpha
- ☐ c. Beta
- ☐ d. All of them are affected

146 Which of the following shields would best protect a person from all three types of radiation?

☐ a. A thick copper screen
☐ b. A thick lead screen
☐ c. A thick aluminium screen
☐ d. A thin lead screen

147 In which of the following is radioactivity not used?

☐ a. Smoke detectors
☐ b. Tracers in medicine
☐ c. Microwave ovens
☐ d. Sterilizing

148 During nuclear fission in a power station, which particle is used to split the uranium nuclei?

☐ a. Proton
☐ b. Neutron
☐ c. Electron
☐ d. Alpha particle

149 What is the function of a moderator in a nuclear power station?

☐ a. To speed up the neutrons
☐ b. To shield the workers
☐ c. To slow down the neutrons
☐ d. To act as a coolant

150 When an atom of uranium is split by a neutron in a nuclear power station, more neutrons are released which may split other uranium atoms. What is this type of reaction called?

☐ a. Fusion reaction
☐ b. Chemical reaction
☐ c. Chain reaction
☐ d. Oxidation reaction

Design and Technology

Questions

1 What is the purpose of a resistor?

- [ ] a. To limit current
- [ ] b. To store energy
- [ ] c. To generate heat
- [ ] d. To increase current

2 What is a capacitor used for?

- [ ] a. Switching a circuit from one state to another
- [ ] b. Increasing voltage
- [ ] c. Storing charge
- [ ] d. Decreasing voltage

3 What is the velocity ratio of a pulley system when the driver pulley is 5 mm in diameter and the driven pulley is 20mm in diameter?

- [ ] a. 4 to 1
- [ ] b. 5 to 20
- [ ] c. 1 to 4
- [ ] d. 2 to 1

4 What is the gear ratio of a system which has a drive gear with 20 teeth driving a gear with 100 teeth?

- [ ] a. 2 to 1
- [ ] b. 1 to 5
- [ ] c. 1 to 2
- [ ] d. 5 to 1

5 What notation does the binary counting system use?

- [ ] a. 1's and 10's
- [ ] b. 2's
- [ ] c. 10's and 100's
- [ ] d. 1's and 0's

6 What is the voltage (potential difference) in a circuit when the current is 40 amps and the resistance is 4 ohms?

- [ ] a. 160 volts
- [ ] b. 80 volts
- [ ] c. 10 volts
- [ ] d. 36 volts

7 When referring to logic gates, what will cause an output through an OR gate?

- [ ] a. When there is an input from one or more inputs
- [ ] b. When there is no input from any source

☐ c. When neither input is positive
☐ d. When there is an input from one or more inputs but not all at the same time

8 What is a LED?

☐ a. Lense entry dial
☐ b. Light entry dial
☐ c. Light emitting diode
☐ d. Light entry diode

9 A teacher wired a circuit to demonstrate how to light a Christmas tree with fairy lights. When the teacher powered the circuit the pupils noted that the lights got dimmer as they went up the tree. Why was this observed?

☐ a. The circuit was wired in series
☐ b. The circuit was wired in parallel
☐ c. The electricity cannot travel far enough to reach the top of the tree
☐ d. One of the bulbs has failed

10 Three resistors of resistance 2 ohms, 4 ohms, and 4 ohms are wired in parallel in an electrical circuit. What is the combined resistance of the circuit?

☐ a. 1 ohm
☐ b. 3.3 ohms
☐ c. 10 ohms
☐ d. 100 ohms

11 A 24-watt, 12-volt headlamp is lit by connecting it to a 12-volt battery of negligible resistance. What is the current flowing?

☐ a. 2 amps
☐ b. 288 amps
☐ c. 24 amps
☐ d. 12 amps

12 A user wishes to develop an electrical circuit which will turn on a light in a room when it gets dark. What electrical component will control this?

☐ a. Thermistor
☐ b. Light dependent resistor
☐ c. Transistor
☐ d. Amplifier

13 What type of circuit is used to change a power supply from a.c. to d.c?

☐ a. Rectifier circuit
☐ b. Transforming circuit
☐ c. Transducing circuit
☐ d. Capacitive circuit

14 What electrical device would you use to switch the voltage from a circuit to one of two motors used to control wiper blades?

☐ a. Capacitor
☐ b. Relay
☐ c. Thermistor
☐ d. Ammeter

15 Why is a digital reading preferred to an analogue reading in some instances?

☐ a. It is easier to use
☐ b. The numbers are bigger
☐ c. It does not fluctuate
☐ d. It is a more accurate reading

Food technology

16 What can a coeliac not eat?

- ☐ a. Products containing gluten
- ☐ b. Nuts
- ☐ c. Eggs
- ☐ d. Dairy products

17 What makes some cuts of meat tougher than others?

- ☐ a. They contain more muscle tissue
- ☐ b. They contain enzymes which do not work
- ☐ c. They contain the proteins collagen and elastin
- ☐ d. The meat is from an older animal

18 Why are raising agents needed to make some food products?

- ☐ a. To produce carbon dioxide to make the food rise
- ☐ b. To react with the protein in the food and make it rise
- ☐ c. To produce oxygen to make the food rise
- ☐ d. To swell and make the food rise

19 Which of the following is not a good source of vitamin D?

- ☐ a. Sunshine
- ☐ b. Margarine
- ☐ c. Tuna
- ☐ d. Carrots

20 What is a sign that you are deficient in vitamin A?

- ☐ a. Scurvy
- ☐ b. Rickets
- ☐ c. Skin problems
- ☐ d. Night blindness

21 What is dextrose?

- ☐ a. Vitamin
- ☐ b. Sugar
- ☐ c. Fat
- ☐ d. Protein

22 How is calcium used by the body?

- ☐ a. To develop bones and teeth
- ☐ b. To help to develop eyesight
- ☐ c. To produce red blood cells
- ☐ d. Control the balance of fluids in the body

23 Why is NSP (dietary fibre) necessary in the diet?

- ☐ a. It provides energy
- ☐ b. It is low in fat
- ☐ c. It increases the speed at which food passes through the body
- ☐ d. It makes you feel full quickly

24 Which of the following contains most dietary fibre?

- ☐ a. Raw carrots
- ☐ b. White rice
- ☐ c. Wholemeal spaghetti
- ☐ d. Bran

25 Which of the following foods would be best for increasing the vitamin C content of a breakfast of cornflakes and milk?

- ☐ a. Swapping whole fat milk for semi-skimmed
- ☐ b. Banana
- ☐ c. Sultanas
- ☐ d. Orange juice

26 When fruit and vegetables are being prepared for processing the cut surfaces can turn brown. This is called enzymic browning. What causes this?

☐ a. Cells being damaged when cut
☐ b. Cells drying out around the areas that have been cut
☐ c. Microbes entering the cut cells
☐ d. Oxygen in the air reacting with the enzymes in the food

27 What is the most effective way to prevent enzymic browning?

☐ a. Cover the food in lemon juice
☐ b. Store food in refrigerator
☐ c. Place the food in water
☐ d. Add sugar to the food

28 What is meant by the term 'disassemble'?

☐ a. To check a product for taste and texture
☐ b. To take a product apart to obtain design information
☐ c. To look at the vitamin content of a food
☐ d. To analyse the amount of fibre present

29 Which of the following foods is a good source of vitamin C?

☐ a. Sunflower oil
☐ b. Eggs
☐ c. Oranges
☐ d. Liver

30 What is vitamin K used for in the human body?

☐ a. Forming healthy teeth and bones
☐ b. Clotting the blood

☐ c. Effective functioning of the reproductive system
☐ d. Promoting good night vision

31 Which of the following recycled materials cannot be used in direct contact with food?

☐ a. Bottles and jars
☐ b. Paper and card
☐ c. Cans
☐ d. Plastics

32 Why should the chef use tongs or wear plastic gloves when handling cooked meats?

☐ a. To avoid contamination
☐ b. To keep the hands clean
☐ c. To avoid mixing flavours
☐ d. To avoid catching a disease

33 Why do fast food outlets use colour-coded equipment in the preparation of food?

☐ a. To make it easy for staff to know what to use
☐ b. To make the preparation area neat and tidy
☐ c. To keep equipment clean
☐ d. To minimise the risk of cross contamination

34 When storing raw and cooked chicken in the same refrigerator where should you store one in relation to the other?

☐ a. Cooked chicken below the raw
☐ b. Same shelf as each other
☐ c. Raw chicken above the cooked
☐ d. Raw chicken on a lower shelf than the cooked

35 The process of identifying hazards in the refrigerator is called which one of the following?

☐ a. Refrigerator hazard
☐ b. Stock control
☐ c. Risk assessment
☐ d. Hazard analysis

36 Salmonella bacteria can cause food poisoning. Which food source is most likely to contain this type of bacteria?

☐ a. Paté
☐ b. Soft cheeses
☐ c. Raw eggs
☐ d. Rice dishes

37 What is a high-risk food preparation area?

☐ a. An area where food is likely to be contaminated by food poisoning bacteria
☐ b. An area where it is crucial to prevent contamination of food by food poisoning bacteria
☐ c. An area where the food is likely to be contaminated by the workers
☐ d. An area where the workers are likely to be contaminated by food poisoning bacteria

38 What is a low-risk food preparation area?

☐ a. An area where the workers will not be contaminated by bacteria
☐ b. An area where the food will not be contaminated by the workers
☐ c. An area where the aim is to minimise bacterial contamination
☐ d. An area where the ingredients used are safe

39 Which act provides protection to consumers against goods that contain false or misleading statements?

☐ a. The Sale of Goods Act (1994)
☐ b. The Consumer Protection Act (1987)
☐ c. The Weights and Measures Act (1985)
☐ d. The Food Labelling Regulations Act (1996)

40 What do the letters CCP mean with regard to food technology?

☐ a. Critical control point
☐ b. Chiller cabinet product
☐ c. Cross contaminated product
☐ d. Cook-chill product

41 Which method of production would you use to produce a wedding cake?

☐ a. One off
☐ b. Repetitive flow
☐ c. Continuous flow
☐ d. Batch

42 Why are diagrams more useful on packet opening instructions than words?

☐ a. They remove the need to read and understand descriptions
☐ b. They are cheaper to produce
☐ c. They look more attractive
☐ d. They fit better into the limited space on packets

43 Why do food products have tamper-evident tops?

☐ a. To stop oxygen getting in and spoiling the food
☐ b. To ensure that children cannot get into the pack

☐ c. To stop people taking food from the pack and putting it back on the shelf
☐ d. To ensure that the food is not interfered with once packaged

44 Which of the following is **not** a reason to recycle waste?

☐ a. Using the materials more than once extends their usefulness
☐ b. Recycling reduces the amount of waste going into landfill sites
☐ c. Saving resources means less jobs in the packaging industry
☐ d. Recycling helps to protect the environment

45 Why do manufacturers need detailed specifications for ingredients and processes for making a product such as tomato ketchup?

☐ a. Consumers expect the product to taste the same each time they buy it
☐ b. To help with stocktaking
☐ c. New staff at the food processing factory need to be trained quickly
☐ d. To improve the recipe when needed

Textiles

46 At what stage would CAD be used in producing a garment?

☐ a. In a production run
☐ b. During the research process
☐ c. During the design process
☐ d. In the evaluation of product success

47 How can manufacturers be more 'environment-friendly'?

☐ a. They can throw away scrap materials
☐ b. They can use less packaging
☐ c. They can add more allowance to the seams
☐ d. They can use chemical finishing

48 What is finishing used for in fabric manufacturing?

☐ a. It is used to finish the ends of the seams
☐ b. It is used to improve the properties of the fabric
☐ c. It is used to make the fabric more physically attractive
☐ d. It is a system for adding loops to the fabric

49 What colour is the natural material made from hemp?

☐ a. Red
☐ b. Brown
☐ c. Green
☐ d. Yellow

50 Which of the following is a natural fibre?

☐ a. Nylon
☐ b. Cotton
☐ c. Acrylic
☐ d. Polyester

51 Nylon is made from which of the following?

☐ a. Oil and wood
☐ b. Oil
☐ c. Wood pulp
☐ d. Oil and coal

52 Which synthetic fibre would you use in designing blankets and sweaters?

- [ ] a. Acetate
- [ ] b. Polyester
- [ ] c. Rayon
- [ ] d. Acrylic

53 Which of the following properties is not a property of nylon carpet yarn?

- [ ] a. Prevents static
- [ ] b. Resists mildew
- [ ] c. Resists stains
- [ ] d. Resists fire

54 Which of the following is a characteristic of Spandex?

- [ ] a. Waterproof
- [ ] b. Wears out quickly
- [ ] c. Allows up to 500% stretching without breaking
- [ ] d. Strong and rigid

55 Which of the following is not a visual quality check?

- [ ] a. Accurate positioning of buttons
- [ ] b. Washability of fabric
- [ ] c. Accurate positioning of belt loops
- [ ] d. Finished ends of seams

56 What is risk assessment used for in industry?

- [ ] a. It ensures that damage will happen
- [ ] b. It is a way of assessing costs
- [ ] c. It is a way of ensuring danger
- [ ] d. It is a system for controlling risks

57 What does performing a risk assessment involve?

- [ ] a. Thinking about ways to speed up production
- [ ] b. Checking the age of workers
- [ ] c. Checking each stage of the manufacturing process for hazards
- [ ] d. Counting the number of products produced per hour

58 What are fabrics not tested for in a safety check?

- [ ] a. The intensity of the coloured dye
- [ ] b. Abrasion
- [ ] c. Strength
- [ ] d. Water resistance

59 Which of the following is not true of safety systems?

- [ ] a. They are used to ensure that raw materials are suitable for the intended product
- [ ] b. They are used to ensure that seams are neat and finished
- [ ] c. They are used to reduce risks
- [ ] d. They are used to ensure that manufacturers make safe products

Graphics and design

60 Anthropometrics is the study of what?

- [ ] a. People's integration into the environment
- [ ] b. Human dimensions
- [ ] c. Colour theory
- [ ] d. Polymers and plastics

61 What shape is seen when you view a circle from an angle of 30°?

- ☐ a. Cylinder
- ☐ b. Circle
- ☐ c. Ellipse
- ☐ d. Eclipse

62 How many vanishing points would you expect to have when producing a two-point perspective drawing?

- ☐ a. 4
- ☐ b. 1
- ☐ c. 2
- ☐ d. 3

63 What drawing technique is used by architects and designers to produce 3D drawings of environments and building plans?

- ☐ a. Orthographic
- ☐ b. Perspective
- ☐ c. Axonometric
- ☐ d. Isometric

64 If a scale of 2:1 was written on a drawing to what size would this be drawn?

- ☐ a. Half size
- ☐ b. Twice full size
- ☐ c. A4
- ☐ d. A3

65 What would be the most suitable scale for modelling a house?

- ☐ a. 1:5
- ☐ b. 1:500
- ☐ c. 1:5,000
- ☐ d. 1:50

66 British Standard for dimensioning of a drawing requires what unit of measurement to be used?

- ☐ a. in (inches)
- ☐ b. mm
- ☐ c. m
- ☐ d. cm

67 Pencils are graded into both hard and soft categories. Which letter or group of letters describe a soft pencil?

- ☐ a. HB
- ☐ b. B
- ☐ c. S
- ☐ d. H

68 From which point on a drawing should dimensions be read?

- ☐ a. Top right hand side
- ☐ b. Bottom left hand side
- ☐ c. Bottom right hand side
- ☐ d. Top left hand side

69 What are the dimensions in mm of a piece of A3 paper?

- ☐ a. 594 × 420
- ☐ b. 594 × 841
- ☐ c. 297 × 211
- ☐ d. 421 × 297

70 Which printing process is commonly used for the production of posters and magazines?

- ☐ a. Flexography
- ☐ b. Gravure
- ☐ c. Screenprinting
- ☐ d. Lithography

71 How long does it take on average for plastic to biodegrade?

- ☐ a. 10–15 years
- ☐ b. 40–50 years
- ☐ c. 25–35 years
- ☐ d. 20–30 years

72 What is a design 'situation'?

- ☐ a. Specification
- ☐ b. Design problem
- ☐ c. Research to be undertaken
- ☐ d. Statement of your intention

73 Which statement best describes the term 'quality control'?

- ☐ a. That a product conforms to British Standard
- ☐ b. The approach which ensures high standards of quality throughout a company
- ☐ c. Inspecting a sample of items at different stages of manufacture
- ☐ d. The acceptable deviation from the ideal size

74 Name an input device which will enable information to be entered into a CAD system?

- ☐ a. Plotter
- ☐ b. Modem
- ☐ c. Printer
- ☐ d. Scanner

75 Which type of mechanism changes rotary motion to reciprocating motion?

- ☐ a. Cam
- ☐ b. Bevel gear
- ☐ c. Lever
- ☐ d. Linkage

Materials and manufacturing

76 When joining two pieces of mild steel together on a permanent basis, which process would be used?

- ☐ a. Soft soldering
- ☐ b. Silver soldering
- ☐ c. Welding
- ☐ d. Brazing

77 Often a manufacturer will use a 'jig' to assist in the manufacture of a product. What is a 'jig'?

- ☐ a. A marking out tool
- ☐ b. A handtool
- ☐ c. A holding device
- ☐ d. A former or mould

78 Which of the following tools would be used for marking out on metal?

- ☐ a. Bradawl
- ☐ b. Scriber
- ☐ c. Marking gauge
- ☐ d. Tin snips

79 Constant working and beating of metal causes strain on the material and it becomes 'work hardened'. Which process can be used to resoften the metal?

- ☐ a. Pickling
- ☐ b. Planishing
- ☐ c. Annealing
- ☐ d. Case hardening

80 Why is unprotected mild steel not suitable for outdoor use?

☐ a. It will discolour
☐ b. It is a ferrous metal and therefore it is magnetic
☐ c. It is a ferrous metal and therefore it will rust
☐ d. It will melt in sunlight

81 Some plastics are said to have a memory; that is they will return to their original shape when heated. Which group of plastics have this so-called 'memory'?

☐ a. Polymers
☐ b. Elastomers
☐ c. Thermoset plastic
☐ d. Thermoplastic

82 What is the correct name for MDF?

☐ a. Mild drawn filamentboard
☐ b. Medium density fibreboard
☐ c. Medium density filamentboard
☐ d. Mild density fibreboard

83 A manufacturer wishes to produce a suntan lotion bottle for a cosmetics company. What process would be used to make the bottle?

☐ a. Extrusion
☐ b. Blow moulding
☐ c. Vacuum forming
☐ d. Injection moulding

84 Many houses today have uPVC double glazed windows. What process would be used to produce the frames for these uPVC windows?

☐ a. Compression moulding
☐ b. Calendering
☐ c. Extrusion
☐ d. Injection moulding

85 Making curves in wood can be problematic. Simply cutting from solid wood causes weaknesses. Which process could be used to overcome this and produce curved wood?

☐ a. Drawing
☐ b. Planishing
☐ c. Laminating
☐ d. Distortion

86 Batch production is best described by which of the following statements?

☐ a. Production of relatively small numbers of products, with tasks being carried out in 'groups'
☐ b. Production of a single product
☐ c. Production of a small number of products on a continuous basis
☐ d. Production of a large number of the same product on a continuous basis

87 A manufacturer will produce 100 plastic food containers for a buffet meal. To make these trays cost effective, which process should be used?

☐ a. Vacuum forming
☐ b. Extrusion
☐ c. Injection moulding
☐ d. Blow moulding

88 A lever is a mechanism which makes an operation easier to perform, for example a door handle or a spanner. All levers fall into separate categories or classes. To what class do scissors belong?

☐ a. First class
☐ b. Fourth class
☐ c. Second class
☐ d. Third class

89 What type of force is applied to unscrew a jam jar lid?

☐ a. Shear
☐ b. Tension
☐ c. Compression
☐ d. Torsion

90 Every operation has an input … and output: What is the missing word?

☐ a. Reaction
☐ b. Access
☐ c. Process
☐ d. Development

Information and Communication Technology

Questions

General ICT

1 What is feedback?

- [ ] a. A cycle of sensing, processing, and reaction
- [ ] b. A fetch, decode, and execute cycle
- [ ] c. A cycle of logging and processing
- [ ] d. A computer program

2 Which of the following is an example of a control system that uses information technology?

- [ ] a. Traffic lights
- [ ] b. A customer database
- [ ] c. A sound file
- [ ] d. An animation

3 What is a manual system?

- [ ] a. The computer operator transferring disk packs
- [ ] b. A system using punched cards
- [ ] c. A system that does not involve the use of IT
- [ ] d. The user instruction manual

Software

4 Which of these is not an example of generic software?

- [ ] a. Graphics package
- [ ] b. File compression software
- [ ] c. Web page editor
- [ ] d. Spreadsheet package

5 What type of application mathematically stores a graphical relationship between parts of the objects?

- [ ] a. CAM
- [ ] b. CAD
- [ ] c. Pixel-based
- [ ] d. Graphics

6 Which of these is a bitmap format file?

- [ ] a. Windows metafile (WMF)
- [ ] b. Encapsulated postscript (EPS)
- [ ] c. Tagged image file (TIF)
- [ ] d. Computer graphics metafile (CGM)

7 What does the file type JPG stand for?

- [ ] a. Joystick port for games
- [ ] b. Java processed graphic
- [ ] c. Joint photographic expert group
- [ ] d. Justified photoimage graphic

8 In business applications, why should we use a computer system?

- [ ] a. To ensure manual workers are no longer required
- [ ] b. To use new technology
- [ ] c. To save time and money
- [ ] d. To create jobs

9 What does a parity check involve?

- [ ] a. Adding an extra 1 or 0 to a binary pattern
- [ ] b. Making sure there are the same number of 0s and 1s in a binary pattern
- [ ] c. Adding up the 1s in a pattern to make sure there are more than 4
- [ ] d. Making sure there is an even number of 0s and 1s

10 What is the term used for adding data from a database into the gaps in a standard letter?

- [ ] a. Mail merge
- [ ] b. Indexing
- [ ] c. Verification
- [ ] d. Validation

11 Which would be the best query to use with a database to find all cars that are white and cost £8000 or less?

- [ ] a. Query car_file.price≤8000 AND car_file.colour='white'
- [ ] b. Query car_file.price<8000 AND car_file.colour='white'
- [ ] c. Query car_file.price<8000 AND car_file.colour=white
- [ ] d. Query car_file.price<8000 OR car_file.colour='white'

12 In which application is a frame used as a guide for inserting text and graphics?

- [ ] a. Desktop publishing
- [ ] b. Database
- [ ] c. Word processing
- [ ] d. Spreadsheet

13 Which package allows the user to manipulate virtually any characteristic of the text and graphics?

- [ ] a. Desktop publishing
- [ ] b. Spreadsheet
- [ ] c. Word processing
- [ ] d. Database

14 What does kerning mean?

- [ ] a. Placing text into columns
- [ ] b. Making sure the last word in a line is pushed as far right as possible
- [ ] c. Adjusting the spacing between characters
- [ ] d. Adjusting the spacing between lines

15 What type of program is a logic bomb?

- [ ] a. Game
- [ ] b. Computer virus

☐ c. E-mail
☐ d. Videoconferencing

16 What program could be described as the backbone of communications for a company?

☐ a. Word processing
☐ b. Desktop publishing
☐ c. Electronic mail
☐ d. Videoconferencing

17 Which of the following is a disadvantage when using e-mail?

☐ a. A group of people may receive the same message
☐ b. An image file may be attached
☐ c. Messages are quicker to arrive than postage mail
☐ d. Messages may not be read if the receiver is busy

18 What does the term 'sans' in comic sans mean?

☐ a. Without tails
☐ b. Funny letters
☐ c. Italic and smaller
☐ d. Unlike Arial

19 What type of software is very popular with home computer users?

☐ a. Computer games
☐ b. FTP
☐ c. Videoconferencing
☐ d. Business graphics

20 What do you call a computer program that recreates the experience of driving a racing car around a track?

☐ a. Vector graphics
☐ b. An automated input device
☐ c. A simulation
☐ d. A robot

21 Which of the following is true of virtual memory?

☐ a. It makes it appear that the computer has more memory by using disk space
☐ b. It is another name for multi-tasking
☐ c. It means parallel processing
☐ d. It allows several printers to be connected to the same computer

22 What are registers?

☐ a. Areas used by the computer operating system
☐ b. Tables of computer programs
☐ c. Checked when shared printing
☐ d. Special types of disk

23 What does firewall software do?

☐ a. Prevents the downloading of software from the Internet
☐ b. Stops access to adult Internet sites
☐ c. Stops viruses entering a computer
☐ d. Prevents hackers remotely accessing a computer

24 What do most URLs start with?

☐ a. htp//:www
☐ b. http://www
☐ c. http//:www
☐ d. http\\:www

25 What does WAP stand for?

☐ a. Wireless application protocol
☐ b. Windows application processing
☐ c. Wide area phone
☐ d. Web access phone

26 Which of the following is not true of simulations?

☐ a. There is no damage to equipment
☐ b. They can recreate the pressures one experiences in a real-life situation
☐ c. Modifications can be made easily
☐ d. People are not in any danger

27 Which of the following is an example of multimedia software?

☐ a. Sound card software
☐ b. DVD
☐ c. CD-ROM encyclopedia
☐ d. Videocard driver

28 What does the network operating system do?

☐ a. Perform hardware tests to determine potential faults
☐ b. Control printer sharing to avoid dual requests between computers
☐ c. Control the file access requests from each computer on the network
☐ d. Control the processes of communication between computers

29 What is the operating system for?

☐ a. To provide the computer with the ability to manage all its own operations
☐ b. To notify the user of any terminal errors
☐ c. To allow the user to use Windows
☐ d. To protect the information stored on the system

30 Which of the following is not a function of the operating system?

☐ a. System of priorities
☐ b. Interfaces with hardware
☐ c. Databases
☐ d. Memory management

31 Which of these functions is not carried out by an operating system?

☐ a. Preventing unauthorized access to the system
☐ b. Managing the transfer of data to a backing storage device
☐ c. Allocating memory space to programs
☐ d. Conversion of analogue to digital signals

32 What does a multi-user operating system do?

☐ a. Allocates each terminal a fraction of the processing time at any given moment
☐ b. Gives each terminal in turn a small amount of processing time
☐ c. Gives unlimited access to processor time
☐ d. Allows two or more programs to run at the same time

33 What is a bootstrap?

☐ a. A loader program
☐ b. Timesharing system
☐ c. Multimode operating system
☐ d. Real time

34 If file compression software like Winzip is used on files with a total size of 90 megabytes, what might be a typical final size after compression?

- [ ] a. 35 megabytes
- [ ] b. 10 megabytes
- [ ] c. 50 kilobytes
- [ ] d. 70 megabytes

35 Which of these is a software-only platform?

- [ ] a. Linux
- [ ] b. MacOS
- [ ] c. Windows 2000
- [ ] d. Java

36 Which of these presentation graphics insertions will normally take up the smallest storage space?

- [ ] a. WMF file
- [ ] b. JPG file
- [ ] c. BMP file
- [ ] d. MID file

37 Which of the following is not a high-level language?

- [ ] a. Visual Basic
- [ ] b. C++
- [ ] c. Mnemonics
- [ ] d. Delphi

38 Which of the following represents a hierarchical structure?

- [ ] a. Stack
- [ ] b. Root
- [ ] c. Terminal nodes
- [ ] d. A tree

39 Which of the listed techniques can be used to design computer programs?

- [ ] a. EBCDIC
- [ ] b. Mnemonic code
- [ ] c. Pseudo code, flow charts, and algorithms
- [ ] d. Reduced instruction set computer

40 What is the machine code equivalent of an entire high-level program called?

- [ ] a. Interpreter code
- [ ] b. Object code
- [ ] c. Assembly code
- [ ] d. Compiled code

41 Which of the following is not an example of system security?

- [ ] a. Antivirus software
- [ ] b. File encryption
- [ ] c. Automated burglar alarm
- [ ] d. System backup

42 In which program are you likely to meet VLOOKUP, INDEX, and SUM?

- [ ] a. Word processing
- [ ] b. DTP
- [ ] c. Database
- [ ] d. Spreadsheet

43 Which of the following is not a spreadsheet function?

- [ ] a. AVERAGE
- [ ] b. MAX
- [ ] c. COUNT
- [ ] d. ADD

44 Which of these formulae is used for working out the average of ten numbers in cells A1 to A10 of a spreadsheet column?

- [ ] a. AVERAGE(A1,A10)
- [ ] b. AVERAGE(A1-A10)
- [ ] c. AVERAGE(A1:A10)
- [ ] d. AVERAGE:(A1,A10)

45 Which of the following is an example of a graphical user interface?

- ☐ a. Windows
- ☐ b. Modem
- ☐ c. DTP
- ☐ d. DOS

46 When using DOS, what is the command for copying a text file called sample1 from the C-drive to a floppy disk?

- ☐ a. C:\DOS\>copy C:\sample1.txt A:\
- ☐ b. C:\DOS\>copy sample1.txt A:\
- ☐ c. C:\DOS\>copy C:\sample1.txt A
- ☐ d. C:\DOS\>copy C:\sample1.txt C:\ A:\

47 In which program would you perform a mail merge?

- ☐ a. DTP
- ☐ b. Database
- ☐ c. Spreadsheet
- ☐ d. Word processing

48 In word processing what do we call the process of vertically aligning the last word of each row?

- ☐ a. Justifying
- ☐ b. Centre aligning
- ☐ c. Left aligning
- ☐ d. Right aligning

Hardware

49 Which of these would be fastest at processing large amounts of data?

- ☐ a. Microcomputer
- ☐ b. Laptop computer
- ☐ c. Mainframe computer
- ☐ d. Minicomputer

50 Which of the following is not true about the use of robots?

- ☐ a. They can carry out repetitive tasks
- ☐ b. They can work in places that would be dangerous to humans
- ☐ c. They are inexpensive to buy and install
- ☐ d. They are more accurate than humans

51 What is an actuator?

- ☐ a. An input device
- ☐ b. A communication device
- ☐ c. A logging device
- ☐ d. An output device

52 Which of these is not needed for videoconferencing?

- ☐ a. Access to an ISDN telephone line
- ☐ b. A multimedia projector
- ☐ c. A microphone or handset
- ☐ d. A digital video camera

53 Which of the following would be of no use in preventing repetitive strain injury (RSI)?

- ☐ a. Using a wrist guard
- ☐ b. A well-positioned keyboard
- ☐ c. Using fewer fingers to type
- ☐ d. Taking frequent breaks

54 What is a physical record?

- ☐ a. How the data is viewed
- ☐ b. Blocking factor
- ☐ c. Information written to or read from a particular device
- ☐ d. The bits in the fields

55 What type of device is MICR?

- [ ] a. Graphics
- [ ] b. Input
- [ ] c. Magnetic store
- [ ] d. Communication

56 Which of the following is a computer input device?

- [ ] a. Plotter
- [ ] b. Mouse
- [ ] c. Printer
- [ ] d. Visual display unit

57 Which of the following is true about the system clock?

- [ ] a. It synchronizes all the chips that do not require synchronizing
- [ ] b. It can be represented by tick tock tick tock
- [ ] c. It is a cause of system crashes
- [ ] d. It is measured in pulses per hour

58 Which of the following is not part of a central processing unit?

- [ ] a. Control unit
- [ ] b. Input and output devices
- [ ] c. Main memory
- [ ] d. Arithmetic and logic unit

59 Which of the following companies made the early ZX Spectrum personal computer?

- [ ] a. IBM
- [ ] b. Apple
- [ ] c. Microsoft
- [ ] d. Sinclair

60 Which of the following is not a type of memory?

- [ ] a. Core store
- [ ] b. MICR
- [ ] c. Semiconductor memory
- [ ] d. EPROM

61 Which of the following is a type of volatile memory?

- [ ] a. RAM
- [ ] b. EPROM
- [ ] c. PROM
- [ ] d. ROM

62 Which of the following are types of network topology?

- [ ] a. Waves and pulses
- [ ] b. Bus, star, and ring
- [ ] c. Digital signals
- [ ] d. Hook, circle, and wire

63 What does LAN stand for?

- [ ] a. Language
- [ ] b. Limited access number
- [ ] c. Local area network
- [ ] d. Linked analogue nesting

64 What does MODEM stand for?

- [ ] a. Modern e-mail processor
- [ ] b. Mode manager
- [ ] c. Modulation-demodulation
- [ ] d. Modelling emulator

65 Which of the following is not true about connecting computers in a local area network?

- [ ] a. Machines do not need their own hard disk
- [ ] b. Users are not affected by file server faults

☐ c. Peripheral devices can be shared

☐ d. Work can be stored centrally

66 What are peripherals that produce hard copy usually known as?

☐ a. CD-ROM writers
☐ b. Chain printers
☐ c. Printers
☐ d. DVD players

67 In what form is the output produced by COM?

☐ a. CD-ROMs
☐ b. Monitors and VDUs
☐ c. Microfilm and microfiche
☐ d. Heat-sensitive paper

68 What does the term MIDI stand for?

☐ a. Menu input driven interface
☐ b. Monitor interference decoding instrument
☐ c. Multimedia integrated digital inventory
☐ d. Musical instrument digital interface

69 Which of the following is true about a backing store device?

☐ a. It can only be used on the computer by which it was created
☐ b. It can store data that can be used by other machines
☐ c. It cannot be written to
☐ d. It can only store computer programs

70 Which of these storage devices does **not** allow direct access?

☐ a. Floppy disk
☐ b. CD-ROM
☐ c. Magnetic tape
☐ d. DVD

Data

71 Which of the following is not a component of a data flow diagram?

☐ a. Data stores
☐ b. Processes
☐ c. Data flows
☐ d. Normalization

72 What is non-interactive processing usually called?

☐ a. Real time processing
☐ b. Batch processing
☐ c. Time sharing
☐ d. Virtual machine

73 What term do we use for pictures that can be manipulated on a computer?

☐ a. Photographs
☐ b. Graphics
☐ c. Paint
☐ d. Animated gifs

74 What two components do we need to create information?

☐ a. Input and output
☐ b. Data and processes
☐ c. Programs and output
☐ d. Databases and programs

75 Which of the following shows the most common data processing operations to be carried out on basic data structures?

- ☐ a. Searching, sorting, merging, reporting
- ☐ b. Addition, deletion, sorting, searching, amending
- ☐ c. Addition, sorting, deletion, amending, creating
- ☐ d. Creation, deletion, searching, reporting

76 Using coded values when checking data reduces the risk of what?

- ☐ a. Verification errors
- ☐ b. Transposition errors
- ☐ c. Validation errors
- ☐ d. Spelling errors

77 What is a DBMS?

- ☐ a. Data management system
- ☐ b. Database management system
- ☐ c. Digital manipulation system
- ☐ d. Direct management system

78 What do we call a linked and organized collection of one or more related files?

- ☐ a. Database
- ☐ b. Data
- ☐ c. Data collection
- ☐ d. Databus

79 Which of the following is not a type of file?

- ☐ a. Random
- ☐ b. Stack
- ☐ c. Serial
- ☐ d. Indexed sequential

80 Which of the following has the characteristics of typeface and point size?

- ☐ a. Character
- ☐ b. Font
- ☐ c. Data
- ☐ d. Field

81 Which of these items of information is **not** included in a barcode on a supermarket product?

- ☐ a. Price
- ☐ b. Manufacturer of the product
- ☐ c. Country of origin
- ☐ d. A check digit

82 Which of these is an example of a two state or binary system?

- ☐ a. A, B, F
- ☐ b. 0, 1, 2
- ☐ c. 0 V, +5 V, −15 V
- ☐ d. On or off

83 How many bits are there in a byte?

- ☐ a. 32
- ☐ b. 64
- ☐ c. 16
- ☐ d. 8

84 Which of these is not a type of hyperlink?

- ☐ a. GOTO
- ☐ b. HTTP
- ☐ c. MAILTO
- ☐ d. FTP

85 Why do we need to validate and verify information?

- ☐ a. To amend records
- ☐ b. To confirm accuracy of data

c. To ensure interactive updating

d. To check field types

86 What is a one-dimensional array?

a. A linear list

b. A register

c. A table

d. A file

87 Which of the following is not a type of sort?

a. Shell

b. Bubble

c. Linear

d. Insertion

88 What is the logical view?

a. The way in which the data is split by the programmer

b. Data read from a device

c. Variable length records

d. Volatility of data

Stepping back from ICT

89 Which of the following generally does not use an IT system?

a. Maintaining pupil records in a school

b. Controlling the population of rabbits

c. Running the National Lottery

d. Analysing radio telescope data in the search for extra-terrestrials

90 Which of these jobs is the computer currently unable to perform?

a. Assembly line work

b. Computer hardware design

c. Football player

d. National Lottery administration

91 Which of the following is not true of computers?

a. They can do calculations faster that humans

b. They do not depend on instructions from humans

c. They never need a rest

d. They can store a large amount of information

92 Which of the following is not true of using a CAM system in manufacturing?

a. The product design cannot be modified

b. Products can be made with great accuracy

c. Waste is kept to a minimum

d. Mass production is much cheaper

93 Which of the following requires real-time processing?

a. Electricity bill distribution

b. Company payroll processing

c. Supermarket stock control

d. Standard letter production

94 Which of the following is **not** a serious social or ethical problem caused by use of the Internet?

a. Job losses caused by on-line services

b. Access to illegal pornographic material

c. Publicity by illegal organizations

d. On-line secure banking facilities

95 What was one of the earliest calculating aids?

- ☐ a. Punched cards
- ☐ b. Slide rule
- ☐ c. Abacus
- ☐ d. Electronic calculator

96 Who invented the difference engine and analytical engines?

- ☐ a. Isaac Newton
- ☐ b. Albert Einstein
- ☐ c. William Oughtred
- ☐ d. Charles Babbage

97 What is the most common use of OMR in the UK?

- ☐ a. Reading the branch code of a bank on a cheque
- ☐ b. Inputting data for the National Lottery
- ☐ c. Barcode reading
- ☐ d. Reading typed postcodes

98 What does EPOS stand for?

- ☐ a. Electrical protection of surge
- ☐ b. Electronic processing on site
- ☐ c. Electronic point of sale
- ☐ d. Enhanced production of sound

99 The Data Protection Act allows access to one's own personal information. Which of the following is an exception?

- ☐ a. Seeing records kept by employers
- ☐ b. Viewing medical records
- ☐ c. Viewing records of financial transactions
- ☐ d. Methods used to detect a crime the person had committed

100 What is the Computer Misuse Act designed to do?

- ☐ a. Prevent illegal downloading of programs
- ☐ b. Prevent access to obscene material
- ☐ c. Prevent software piracy
- ☐ d. Make hacking illegal

History
Questions

1 Which explorer's decision to label his maps of the Great Plains as the 'Great American Desert' discouraged settlers from attempting to settle on the Plains until the 1860s?

- ☐ a. Joseph McCoy
- ☐ b. Brigham Young
- ☐ c. Major Stephen Long
- ☐ d. Lewis and Clarke

2 What was the main reason why the Plains Indians moved around the Great Plains?

- ☐ a. To follow the migrating buffalo herds
- ☐ b. To keep in touch with other tribes
- ☐ c. To keep away from the settlers in their wagon trains
- ☐ d. To avoid attack by the US Army

3 What is involved in the Plains Indian practice of 'counting coup'?

- ☐ a. Stealing a horse
- ☐ b. Counting the warriors in a tribe
- ☐ c. Touching an enemy in battle
- ☐ d. Killing your enemy

4 Where did American Indians hope their spirit would go to after their death?

- ☐ a. Wakan Tanka
- ☐ b. The Great Plains
- ☐ c. The Happy Hunting Ground
- ☐ d. Black Hills

5 Which of these was a push factor that led to settlers travelling across the Plains to California and Oregon in the 1840s?

- ☐ a. Newspaper stories based on the accounts of Mountain Men and Christian missionaries about the West
- ☐ b. Guides such as *The Emigrants' Guide to Oregon and California* published in 1845
- ☐ c. The Pre-emption Bill of 1842
- ☐ d. The economic depression of 1837 in the east of the USA

6 Which eastern city did the Mormons leave from in 1846 at the start of their journey to the Great Salt Lake?

- ☐ a. Nauvoo, Illinois
- ☐ b. Kirtland, Ohio
- ☐ c. Independence, Missouri
- ☐ d. Palmyra, New York State

7 Where in the USA was gold discovered in 1848?

☐ a. The Great Plains
☐ b. Oregon
☐ c. California
☐ d. Texas

8 Where did the Central Pacific Railroad Company and the Union Pacific Railroad Company meet on completion of the trans-continental railroad in 1869?

☐ a. Abilene, Kansas
☐ b. The Little Bighorn River, Montana
☐ c. The American River, California
☐ d. Promontory Point, Utah

9 Which of these is not an act passed by the US Government to encourage homesteaders to settle on the Great Plains?

☐ a. The Desert Land Act, 1877
☐ b. The Homestead Act, 1862
☐ c. The Pre-emption Act, 1842
☐ d. The Timber Culture Act, 1873

10 Which of these solutions to the problems of farming on the Great Plains was not available to the homesteaders by 1880?

☐ a. Turkey Red wheat capable of growing in the harsh conditions
☐ b. Pesticide to kill off swarms of grasshoppers
☐ c. Joseph Glidden's barbed wire to keep animals off the growing crops
☐ d. John Deere's Sodbuster plough to cut through the previously uncultivated Plains soil

11 Which of these men founded the first cow town at Abilene where cattle driven from Texas could be sold to buyers from the eastern states?

☐ a. Joseph McCoy
☐ b. Oliver Loving
☐ c. Charles Goodnight
☐ d. John Illif

12 Which of these American Indian chiefs led a successful war against the US Army and forced the USA to sign a peace treaty on his terms?

☐ a. Red Cloud
☐ b. Big Foot
☐ c. Little Crow
☐ d. Sitting Bull

13 Which of the following famous figures of the American West was not a gun fighter?

☐ a. Buffalo Bill
☐ b. John Wesley Hardin
☐ c. Billy the Kid
☐ d. Wild Bill Hickok

14 Which of the following is not a reason why General Custer and the 7th Cavalry were defeated at the Battle of the Little Bighorn in 1876?

☐ a. The defeat by Crazy Horse of General Crook in the Battle of the Rosebud
☐ b. The decision by Custer to march his men through rather than round the Wolf Mountains on his way to the Indian camp
☐ c. The failure of Colonel Gibbon and General Terry to follow the battle plan agreed with Custer

d. The decision by Custer to ignore his Crow Indian scouts' warnings not to attack the Indian camp

15 Which of these American Indian chiefs did not fight at the Battle of the Little Bighorn in 1876?

a. Sitting Bull
b. Crazy Horse
c. Red Cloud
d. Gall

16 What was the name of the Paiute Holy Man who brought the Ghost Dance movement to the Plains Indians?

a. Sitting Bull
b. Wovoka
c. Big Foot
d. Red Cloud

19th-century British politics

17 Which of these groups did not have the vote after the 1832 Reform Act?

a. County copyholders of land worth over £10 a year
b. County leaseholders of land worth over £50 a year
c. Occupiers of borough properties worth over £10 a year
d. Town workers earning over £20 a year in wages

18 In which city was the Peterloo massacre of 1819?

a. London
b. Birmingham

c. Manchester
d. Liverpool

19 Which of these was not one of the six points of the People's Charter?

a. The payment of members of Parliament
b. A vote for every man over 21 years of age
c. The introduction of secret ballots
d. The abolition of all powers held by the king over Parliament

20 In which year was the Poor Law Amendment Act passed?

a. 1848
b. 1834
c. 1832
d. 1840

21 Which of the following was not part of the 1833 Factory Act?

a. All children working in factories between the ages of 9 and 13 to attend two hours of school a day
b. No child under 9 to work in a factory or mill
c. Adult workers over the age of 18 limited to 14 hours work a day
d. Children between 14 and 18 to work a maximum of 12 hours a day

22 Who led the opposition to the Mines Act of 1842 in the House of Lords?

a. Lord Shaftesbury
b. Lord Londonderry
c. Viscount Castlereagh
d. The Duke of Wellington

23 Which reforming politician was involved with the Ten Hours Movement, the Mines Act of 1842, and the Ragged School Union?

- ☐ a. Michael Sadler
- ☐ b. Samuel Whitbread
- ☐ c. Sir Robert Peel
- ☐ d. Lord Shaftesbury

24 Who was known as the 'Railway King'?

- ☐ a. Richard Trevithick
- ☐ b. William Huskisson
- ☐ c. George Stephenson
- ☐ d. George Hudson

Russia 1917–1945

25 Who became leader of the Provisional Government of Russia after the February Revolution in 1917?

- ☐ a. Leon Trotsky
- ☐ b. Rasputin
- ☐ c. Alexandr Kerensky
- ☐ d. Vladimir Ilych Lenin

26 Which country helped Lenin to return to Russia after the February Revolution?

- ☐ a. Britain
- ☐ b. Germany
- ☐ c. France
- ☐ d. Austria

27 Which of these promises was not part of Lenin's April Thesis in 1917?

- ☐ a. Bread
- ☐ b. Land
- ☐ c. Peace
- ☐ d. War

28 Which treaty ended the involvement of Russia in World War I in 1918?

- ☐ a. Versailles
- ☐ b. Brest-Litovsk
- ☐ c. Moscow
- ☐ d. Locarno

29 What was the name of the economic system introduced by Lenin and the Bolsheviks in 1921 to stabilize the country?

- ☐ a. New Economic Policy
- ☐ b. War Communism
- ☐ c. Collectivization
- ☐ d. Five Year Plan

30 Who became the leader of the Soviet Union after Lenin's death in 1924?

- ☐ a. Grigory Zinoviev
- ☐ b. Lev Kamenev
- ☐ c. Joseph Stalin
- ☐ d. Leon Trotsky

31 What was the name of the body set up to administer the Five Year Plans introduced by Stalin in 1928?

- ☐ a. Gosplan
- ☐ b. Politburo
- ☐ c. Mensheviks
- ☐ d. NKVD

32 Which of the following leading Bolsheviks was not a victim of Stalin's show trials in the 1930s?

- ☐ a. Grigory Zinoviev
- ☐ b. Leon Trotsky
- ☐ c. Lev Kamenev
- ☐ d. Nikolai Bukharin

33 What was the name of the Russian film maker who made propaganda films for the Bolsheviks such as 'The Battleship Potemkin'?

☐ a. Sergei Kirov
☐ b. Lavrenti Beria
☐ c. Joseph Goebbels
☐ d. Sergei Eisenstein

34 Why was Alexei Stakhanov hailed as a hero of the workers of the Soviet Union?

☐ a. He worked on the construction of the Moscow Metro
☐ b. He led the Workers' Council in his steel factory
☐ c. He encouraged workers to send gifts to Stalin and the other Soviet leaders
☐ d. He worked extremely hard and exceeded the production targets in his coal mine

35 Which job did Stalin hold in the Communist Party from 1922 that allowed him to place his supporters in powerful positions?

☐ a. Head of the Secret Police
☐ b. President
☐ c. War Minister
☐ d. General Secretary

36 Which region of the Soviet Union suffered a famine from 1930 that killed over 5 million people as a result of Stalin's forced policy of Collectivization?

☐ a. Georgia
☐ b. Siberia
☐ c. Armenia
☐ d. Ukraine

37 Which city's name was changed to Leningrad in honour of the first leader of the Soviet Union?

☐ a. Moscow
☐ b. St Petersburg
☐ c. Kiev
☐ d. Minsk

38 Which group was blamed by Stalin for the disasters caused by the Collectivization policies?

☐ a. Kulaks
☐ b. Whites
☐ c. Soldiers
☐ d. Church

39 What was the name of the official newspaper of the Soviet Union used to spread propaganda for the government?

☐ a. Kulak
☐ b. Pravda
☐ c. Gosplan
☐ d. Workers' News

World War I

40 Which of these countries was not a member of the Triple Alliance?

☐ a. Turkey
☐ b. Austria-Hungary
☐ c. Italy
☐ d. Germany

41 Which of these countries was not a member of the Triple Entente?

☐ a. Britain
☐ b. France
☐ c. USA
☐ d. Russia

42 Over which country were Germany and France in dispute during the Agadir Crisis of 1911?

- [ ] a. Egypt
- [ ] b. Turkey
- [ ] c. Morocco
- [ ] d. Algeria

43 In which region of Europe were there two wars between 1912 and 1913?

- [ ] a. Balkans
- [ ] b. Russia and France
- [ ] c. Italy
- [ ] d. Germany

44 What was the nationality of Gavrilo Princip, the member of the Black Hand who shot Archduke Franz Ferdinand in Sarajevo in June 1914?

- [ ] a. Serbian
- [ ] b. Turkish
- [ ] c. Russian
- [ ] d. Bosnian

45 Because of the invasion of which country did Britain declare war on Germany on 4 August 1914?

- [ ] a. Belgium
- [ ] b. France
- [ ] c. Holland
- [ ] d. Serbia

46 What was the name given to the German plan to invade and defeat France?

- [ ] a. Hindenburg Plan
- [ ] b. Plan 17
- [ ] c. Schlieffen Plan
- [ ] d. Kaiser Plan

47 Which of these places did not see a major battle on the Western Front in 1914?

- [ ] a. Mons
- [ ] b. Verdun
- [ ] c. Ypres
- [ ] d. The Marne

48 Where was poison gas first used by the Germans in World War I?

- [ ] a. Second Battle of Ypres, 1915
- [ ] b. Battle of the Somme, 1916
- [ ] c. Battle of the Marne, 1914
- [ ] d. Battle of Loos, 1915

49 Which of the following was not part of the Defence of the Realm Act introduced in Britain in 1914?

- [ ] a. Censorship of newspapers
- [ ] b. Government control of key industries
- [ ] c. Changes to pub opening times
- [ ] d. Abolition of Trade Unions

50 When was conscription introduced in Britain?

- [ ] a. 1914
- [ ] b. There was no conscription in World War I
- [ ] c. 1916
- [ ] d. 1918

51 Which country was under attack in the Gallipoli Campaign in 1915?

- [ ] a. Italy
- [ ] b. Germany
- [ ] c. Austria-Hungary
- [ ] d. Turkey

52 Which British field marshal famously appeared on a recruiting poster pointing at the reader with the words 'Britain wants you, Join your country's army, God Save the King'?

- [ ] a. Sir John French
- [ ] b. Sir Henry Rawlinson
- [ ] c. Lord Kitchener
- [ ] d. Sir Douglas Haig

53 Which of these is the only country that actually saw a military battle on its own soil in World War I?

- [ ] a. Britain
- [ ] b. Germany
- [ ] c. USA
- [ ] d. Russia

54 Which of these World War I pilots shot down the most enemy planes?

- [ ] a. Robert Little
- [ ] b. Manfred Von Richthofen
- [ ] c. Albert Ball
- [ ] d. Rene Fonck

55 What was the name of the initially successful campaign by the Russians against Austria-Hungary in June 1916?

- [ ] a. The Danilov Offensive
- [ ] b. The Samsonov Offensive
- [ ] c. The Brusilov Offensive
- [ ] d. The Nicholas II Offensive

56 What was the name of the Russian plan devised by Yuri Danilov in 1910 to attack East Prussia with four armies at the outbreak of war?

- [ ] a. The Schlieffen Plan
- [ ] b. Plan 17
- [ ] c. Plan 19
- [ ] d. The East Prussian Plan

57 What was the name of the two territories taken from France after the Franco-Prussian war of 1870 that caused long-term tensions between the two nations?

- [ ] a. Belgium and Luxembourg
- [ ] b. Alsace and Luxembourg
- [ ] c. Lorraine and Bavaria
- [ ] d. Alsace and Lorraine

58 In which year did the USA enter World War I?

- [ ] a. 1917
- [ ] b. 1916
- [ ] c. 1918
- [ ] d. 1915

59 Which of these countries was still fighting in World War I on 11 November 1918?

- [ ] a. France
- [ ] b. Austria-Hungary
- [ ] c. Turkey
- [ ] d. Russia

60 Where was the peace treaty with Germany signed at the end of World War I?

- [ ] a. St Germain
- [ ] b. Trianon
- [ ] c. Sevres
- [ ] d. Versailles

61 Who represented the USA at the Versailles Peace Conference?

- [ ] a. David Lloyd-George
- [ ] b. Vittorio Orlando
- [ ] c. George Clemenceau
- [ ] d. Woodrow Wilson

62 Which of these areas of land was not taken away from Germany after World War I?

- ☐ a. Rhineland
- ☐ b. Eupen and Malmedy
- ☐ c. Northern Schleswig
- ☐ d. Alsace and Lorraine

63 Which of these was not one of President Wilson's Fourteen Points?

- ☐ a. Alsace and Lorraine to be returned to France
- ☐ b. Germany to accept total blame for World War I
- ☐ c. The League of Nations to be set up
- ☐ d. Self determination for nationalities in Eastern Europe

64 From which empire did Czechoslovakia emerge after 1919 as an independent nation?

- ☐ a. British
- ☐ b. Turkish
- ☐ c. Russian
- ☐ d. Austro-Hungarian

The Treaty of Versailles and the League of Nations

65 What did Article 231 of the Treaty of Versailles state?

- ☐ a. That Kaiser Wilhelm of Germany abdicate his throne
- ☐ b. That Germany had to return Alsace and Lorraine to France
- ☐ c. That Germany was to blame for the start of World War I
- ☐ d. That no German troops could be stationed in the Rhineland

66 Which of the victorious allied nations was excluded from the peace negotiations at Versailles?

- ☐ a. Russia
- ☐ b. USA
- ☐ c. Italy
- ☐ d. Belgium

67 Whose idea was the setting up of the League of Nations?

- ☐ a. Douglas Haig
- ☐ b. David Lloyd-George
- ☐ c. Woodrow Wilson
- ☐ d. Lenin

68 Which of these countries never joined the League of Nations?

- ☐ a. USA
- ☐ b. Soviet Union
- ☐ c. Japan
- ☐ d. Germany

69 Which of these League of Nations bodies was responsible for deciding on border disputes between member states?

- ☐ a. World Health Organization
- ☐ b. International Labour Organization
- ☐ c. Secretariat
- ☐ d. Permanent Court of Justice

70 Under which of the following treaties did Germany accept the western borders imposed by the Treaty of Versailles?

- ☐ a. Rapallo Treaty
- ☐ b. Dawes Plan
- ☐ c. Geneva Protocol
- ☐ d. Locarno Treaties

71 Which independent African nation did Mussolini invade in 1935?

- ☐ a. Manchuria
- ☐ b. Abyssinia
- ☐ c. Libya
- ☐ d. Albania

72 Who did the League of Nations send to Manchuria to investigate the Japanese invasion of 1931?

- ☐ a. Lord Curzon
- ☐ b. Lord Halifax
- ☐ c. Lord Lytton
- ☐ d. Lord Keynes

73 What was the response of the Japanese Government to the demands of the League of Nations for Japan to withdraw from Manchuria?

- ☐ a. The Japanese left the League in 1933
- ☐ b. The Japanese invited the League of Nations to a conference on Manchuria
- ☐ c. The Japanese apologized for their actions to the League of Nations
- ☐ d. The Japanese withdrew from Manchuria in 1933

74 In which European country was there a brutal civil war between 1936 and 1939 that the League of Nations was powerless to stop?

- ☐ a. France
- ☐ b. Hungary
- ☐ c. Poland
- ☐ d. Spain

75 Where was the headquarters of the League of Nations?

- ☐ a. London
- ☐ b. The Hague
- ☐ c. Paris
- ☐ d. Geneva

76 Which of these statements about the League of Nations is untrue?

- ☐ a. The Assembly and the Council were unable to act unless decisions were unanimous
- ☐ b. The League was weakened by the failure of the USA to join
- ☐ c. The League made no attempt to stop Mussolini's invasion of Abyssinia
- ☐ d. The League had no armed forces of its own

Weimar Republic/Nazi Germany

77 Which region of Germany was demilitarized as a result of the Treaty of Versailles in 1919?

- ☐ a. Alsace and Lorraine
- ☐ b. East Prussia
- ☐ c. The Rhineland
- ☐ d. Danzig

78 Who was the first president of the Weimar Republic?

- ☐ a. Stresemann
- ☐ b. Ebert
- ☐ c. Hitler
- ☐ d. Hindenburg

79 Which group of Germans was referred to as the 'November Criminals'?

☐ a. The Freikorps
☐ b. The Spartacists
☐ c. The signatories of the Treaty of Versailles
☐ d. The Nazi Party

80 Which two countries occupied the Ruhr in 1923 to force the Germans to pay the reparations demanded by the Treaty of Versailles?

☐ a. Belgium and France
☐ b. Britain and Holland
☐ c. Poland and Belgium
☐ d. Russia and France

81 Where did the Nazis attempt a coup in 1923?

☐ a. Weimar
☐ b. Danzig
☐ c. Munich
☐ d. Berlin

82 Which German politician ended the occupation of the Ruhr, accepted the Dawes Plan, introduced a new stable currency and signed the Locarno Settlement?

☐ a. Paul Hindenburg
☐ b. Gustav Stresemann
☐ c. Adolf Hitler
☐ d. Friedrich Ebert

83 Which of these Nazi Party leaders was killed during the Night of the Long Knives on 30 June 1934?

☐ a. Joseph Goebbels
☐ b. Heinrich Himmler
☐ c. Ernst Rohm
☐ d. Hermann Goering

84 When was Hitler appointed Chancellor of Germany?

☐ a. 1923
☐ b. 1929
☐ c. 1936
☐ d. 1933

85 Under which 1933 law did Hitler and the Nazis assume dictatorial powers over Germany?

☐ a. The Nazi Bill
☐ b. The Hitler Bill
☐ c. The Enabling Bill
☐ d. The Reichstag Bill

86 What was the name of the Nazi secret police?

☐ a. SS
☐ b. Gestapo
☐ c. SA
☐ d. Freikorps

87 How did Hitler break the Treaty of Versailles in 1938?

☐ a. Militarization of the Rhineland
☐ b. Withdrawal from the League of Nations
☐ c. Introduction of conscription
☐ d. Anschluss with Austria

88 What did Hitler hope to achieve through his policy of *Lebensraum*?

☐ a. Protection of the rights of German workers
☐ b. Freedom from the terms of the Treaty of Versailles
☐ c. Peaceful relations with Eastern Europe
☐ d. Living space in the east of Europe for the Germans

89 Which of these anti-Jewish laws was not introduced in the Nuremberg Laws of 1935?

☐ a. Jews have to use separate seats on buses and in public parks
☐ b. Jews cannot be German citizens
☐ c. All Jews to live in ghettos
☐ d. No Jew may marry or have sex with a non-Jew

90 Which of the following did the Nazis introduce to the school curriculum?

☐ a. PE
☐ b. Maths
☐ c. Race studies
☐ d. History

91 What was the name of the organization set up by the Nazis which all boys had to join?

☐ a. Wehrmacht
☐ b. Freikorps
☐ c. Hitler Youth
☐ d. SS

92 What was the name of the organization set up by the Nazis which all girls had to join?

☐ a. Nazi Women
☐ b. Labour Front
☐ c. German Girls Group
☐ d. League of German Maidens

93 With whom did the Nazis sign a treaty in 1939, which had secret clauses carving up Poland between them?

☐ a. Britain
☐ b. Japan
☐ c. Italy
☐ d. The Soviet Union

94 What is the English translation of Hitler's *Mein Kampf*?

☐ a. The Nazi Bible
☐ b. My Ideas
☐ c. My Struggle
☐ d. My Germany

95 Who was the Nazi propaganda Minister?

☐ a. Joseph Goebbels
☐ b. Adolf Hitler
☐ c. Franz von Papen
☐ d. Hermann Goering

96 Where were the Nazi war criminals tried after World War II?

☐ a. Nuremberg
☐ b. Paris
☐ c. Hanover
☐ d. Berlin

World War II

97 In 1938 where was the last meeting held between Britain, France, Italy, and Germany that attempted to prevent war?

☐ a. Stresa
☐ b. Locarno
☐ c. Berlin
☐ d. Munich

98 The invasion of which country by Germany on 1 September 1939 started World War II?

☐ a. Poland
☐ b. France
☐ c. Belgium
☐ d. Czechoslovakia

99 What was the name of the operation that removed over 300,000 British and French troops from Dunkirk in June 1940?

- [ ] a. Operation Overlord
- [ ] b. Operation Sealion
- [ ] c. Operation Dynamo
- [ ] d. Operation Retreat

100 Who became prime minister of Britain in May 1940?

- [ ] a. Neville Chamberlain
- [ ] b. Winston Churchill
- [ ] c. Lord Halifax
- [ ] d. David Lloyd-George

101 Which of these groups of people were evacuated from British cities in September 1939?

- [ ] a. Children
- [ ] b. The King and Queen
- [ ] c. Politicians
- [ ] d. Doctors

102 Whose 1942 report promised a fairer and better society with a full welfare state after the end of the war?

- [ ] a. Winston Churchill
- [ ] b. William Beveridge
- [ ] c. Aneurin Bevan
- [ ] d. Clement Attlee

103 Which Allied commander led the defeat of Rommel's Afrika Korps at the Battle of El Alamein in 1942?

- [ ] a. General Eisenhower
- [ ] b. General Wavell
- [ ] c. General Montgomery
- [ ] d. General Patton

104 Which Soviet city suffered a siege by the Germans from September 1941 to January 1944 in which one million people died?

- [ ] a. Moscow
- [ ] b. Stalingrad
- [ ] c. Leningrad
- [ ] d. Kiev

105 The Japanese surprise attack on Pearl Harbor brought which country into World War II in 1941?

- [ ] a. USA
- [ ] b. Australia
- [ ] c. China
- [ ] d. Canada

106 Which German city was bombed in February 1945 resulting in a firestorm that killed more then 35,000 people?

- [ ] a. Berlin
- [ ] b. Weimar
- [ ] c. Hanover
- [ ] d. Dresden

107 Which of these places hosted the last meeting of the three major wartime allies, Britain, the USSR, and the USA?

- [ ] a. Tehran
- [ ] b. Casablanca
- [ ] c. Potsdam
- [ ] d. Yalta

The Cold War

108 Which of these countries did not benefit from the Marshall Plan?

- [ ] a. Italy
- [ ] b. East Germany
- [ ] c. West Germany
- [ ] d. Greece

109 Which event occurred between 1948 and 1949 when Stalin tried to cut off West Berlin from the outside world?

- [ ] a. Announcement of the Truman Doctrine
- [ ] b. Berlin Airlift
- [ ] c. The dropping of the first atomic bomb
- [ ] d. Building of the Berlin Wall

110 Which of these countries was not behind the 'Iron Curtain'?

- [ ] a. Austria
- [ ] b. Poland
- [ ] c. Czechoslovakia
- [ ] d. Hungary

111 Which country staged an uprising against Soviet control in 1956?

- [ ] a. Rumania
- [ ] b. Czechoslovakia
- [ ] c. Hungary
- [ ] d. East Germany

112 When was the Berlin Wall built?

- [ ] a. 1948
- [ ] b. 1956
- [ ] c. 1953
- [ ] d. 1961

113 Which of these countries did not send troops to fight in the Korean War 1950–53?

- [ ] a. USSR
- [ ] b. USA
- [ ] c. China
- [ ] d. Britain

114 Which US president threatened to invade Cuba if the USSR deployed nuclear missiles there during the Cuban Missile Crisis?

- [ ] a. John F Kennedy
- [ ] b. Harry S Truman
- [ ] c. Ronald Reagan
- [ ] d. Dwight Eisenhower

115 Which of these nations was not a member of NATO?

- [ ] a. Switzerland
- [ ] b. Turkey
- [ ] c. West Germany
- [ ] d. Canada

116 Who replaced Stalin as leader of the USSR in 1953?

- [ ] a. Nikita Khrushchev
- [ ] b. Mikhail Gorbachev
- [ ] c. Leon Trotsky
- [ ] d. Leonid Brezhnev

117 Which doctrine allowed the USSR to intervene in the affairs of communist states to ensure they maintained socialist governments?

- [ ] a. Khrushchev Doctrine
- [ ] b. Truman Doctrine
- [ ] c. Monroe Doctrine
- [ ] d. Brezhnev Doctrine

118 Which US president ended the involvement of US troops in the Vietnam War?

- [ ] a. John F Kennedy
- [ ] b. Jimmy Carter
- [ ] c. Richard Nixon
- [ ] d. Gerald Ford

119 Vietnam was a colony of which European country until 1954?

- [ ] a. Spain
- [ ] b. Britain
- [ ] c. France
- [ ] d. Holland

120 Who became the last leader of the USSR in 1985?

- [ ] a. Yuri Andropov
- [ ] b. Leonid Brezhnev
- [ ] c. Mikhail Gorbachev
- [ ] d. Josef Stalin

121 Which year saw the fall of the Berlin Wall and the overthrow of the communist system in Eastern Europe?

- [ ] a. 1991
- [ ] b. 1985
- [ ] c. 1989
- [ ] d. 1980

122 Which US and Soviet leaders signed the SALT II arms reduction treaty in 1979?

- [ ] a. Nixon and Brezhnev
- [ ] b. Nixon and Khrushchev
- [ ] c. Carter and Brezhnev
- [ ] d. Carter and Khrushchev

Medicine through time

123 For what medical purpose do historians believe that prehistoric people performed trephination operations?

- [ ] a. To remove the brain for use in a religious ceremony
- [ ] b. To treat a patient's flesh wound
- [ ] c. To examine the brain as part of their anatomical research
- [ ] d. To release the evil spirit from the patient's skull

124 Which of the following is not a method historians can use to find out about the medicine of prehistoric peoples?

- [ ] a. Studying tribes living a similar life today
- [ ] b. Studying their written records
- [ ] c. By digging up and examining skeletons
- [ ] d. By studying cave paintings

125 Which of the following was the Egyptian god who gave doctors their ability to heal the sick?

- [ ] a. Taweret
- [ ] b. Sekhmet
- [ ] c. Thoth
- [ ] d. Imhotep

126 Which of the following is a written record of over 700 treatments used by Egyptian doctors?

- [ ] a. Papyrus Sekhmet
- [ ] b. Papyrus Imhotep
- [ ] c. Papyrus Ebers
- [ ] d. Papyrus Tutankhamun

127 What was the Egyptian theory of the body containing a series of channels, which if blocked made the person ill, based on?

- ☐ a. Mummification
- ☐ b. Egyptian gods
- ☐ c. The Egyptian irrigation system
- ☐ d. Trephining

128 Who was the Greek god of healing?

- ☐ a. Asclepios
- ☐ b. Hippocrates
- ☐ c. Galen
- ☐ d. Imhotep

129 Which Ancient Greek doctor encouraged his pupils to use the technique of clinical observation when treating patients?

- ☐ a. Asclepios
- ☐ b. Galen
- ☐ c. Thoth
- ☐ d. Hippocrates

130 What non-religious explanation is there for the recoveries from illness made by many of the visitors to the Asclepion temples in Ancient Greece?

- ☐ a. The night spent sleeping in the open-sided Abaton
- ☐ b. The patients were not ill in the first place
- ☐ c. The use by the priests of the methods of Hippocrates
- ☐ d. The temples encouraged a healthy regime of fitness, cleanliness, and a good diet

131 Why was Claudius Galen wrong about human anatomy?

- ☐ a. Human anatomy changed after Galen's death
- ☐ b. Galen was unable to dissect human bodies so had to work on pigs and dogs
- ☐ c. Galen copied the old ideas of other doctors who were also wrong
- ☐ d. Galen used deformed human corpses

132 Why were Roman cities so clean and healthy when compared to other cites of the next one thousand years?

- ☐ a. The Romans recycled all of their waste
- ☐ b. The Romans built their cities near swamps and dumped their rubbish in these
- ☐ c. The Romans had a highly developed public health system
- ☐ d. The Romans burnt all of their rubbish

133 Which of these is one way that the Catholic Church in Europe helped medicine after the collapse of the Roman Empire?

- ☐ a. The Pope encouraged medical research and dissection
- ☐ b. The monasteries kept collections of the ancient writings of Hippocrates and Galen
- ☐ c. The Church stated that Galen was wrong and encouraged challenges to his work
- ☐ d. The Church sent monks all over the known world to collect new medical ideas

134 What are the four humours?

- [ ] a. Fire, earth, water, and air
- [ ] b. Yellow bile, black bile, blood, and phlegm
- [ ] c. Diagnosis, prognosis, observation, and treatment
- [ ] d. Spring, Summer, Autumn, and Winter

135 Why were Arab doctors such as Avicenna and Rhazes unable to correct Galen's errors on human anatomy?

- [ ] a. All muslims were cremated on the day of their death
- [ ] b. Dissection was forbidden under Islamic law
- [ ] c. They did not have the tools to cut open the bodies
- [ ] d. The doctors were frightened of any new ideas

136 Which Arab doctor showed that blood did not pass through holes in the septum as Galen claimed, over 300 years before Vesalius made the same discovery?

- [ ] a. Rhazes
- [ ] b. Ibn an-Nafis
- [ ] c. Avicenna
- [ ] d. Albucasis

137 In medieval Europe what was believed to be the cure for scrofula?

- [ ] a. Bleeding the patient to restore the body's humours
- [ ] b. Treatment based on a study of the patient's urine
- [ ] c. Amputation by a barber surgeon
- [ ] d. Being touched by a king or queen

138 Which of these factors was not involved in Ambroise Pare's development of a new treatment for gunshot wounds?

- [ ] a. Religion
- [ ] b. War
- [ ] c. Chance
- [ ] d. The role of the individual

139 What did Johannes Gutenberg introduce into Europe in 1454 that helped to spread medical discoveries more quickly?

- [ ] a. The telegraph
- [ ] b. A law forcing doctors to share their knowledge
- [ ] c. The common use of Latin amongst doctors
- [ ] d. The printing press

140 What did William Harvey develop a scientific explanation for in 1616?

- [ ] a. The circulation of blood around the human body
- [ ] b. The power of the human mind
- [ ] c. The spread of bubonic plague
- [ ] d. The causes of disease

141 Who introduced inoculation against smallpox to Britain in 1721?

- [ ] a. Edward Jenner
- [ ] b. Louis Pasteur
- [ ] c. James Simpson
- [ ] d. Lady Wortley Montagu

142 Which disease did Edward Jenner use to vaccinate patients against smallpox?

☐ a. Cholera
☐ b. Typhoid
☐ c. Cowpox
☐ d. Influenza

143 In which year was compulsory vaccination against smallpox introduced?

☐ a. 1875
☐ b. 1832
☐ c. 1848
☐ d. 1853

144 Who wrote the 1842 *Report on the sanitary condition of the labouring population* highlighting the need to clean up the towns of Britain to reduce the high rates of disease and death?

☐ a. Thomas Southwood-Smith
☐ b. William Farr
☐ c. Edwin Chadwick
☐ d. John Snow

145 Which English doctor discovered the link between cholera and dirty water in 1854 by studying an outbreak around Broad Street in London?

☐ a. Edward Jenner
☐ b. Joseph Lister
☐ c. Robert Koch
☐ d. John Snow

146 What was the name of the British Government minister who was responsible for sending Florence Nightingale and her team of nurses to the military hospital at Scutari during the Crimean War in 1854?

☐ a. Edwin Chadwick
☐ b. David Lloyd-George
☐ c. Sidney Herbert
☐ d. William Beveridge

147 What did Louis Pasteur discover in 1861?

☐ a. The link between germs and disease in humans
☐ b. A vaccine for rabies
☐ c. The circulation of blood around the human body
☐ d. Germ theory

148 In which year did a Conservative Government pass a compulsory Public Health Act in Britain, forcing local councils to take action to improve the supply of clean drinking water and sanitation?

☐ a. 1848
☐ b. 1875
☐ c. 1906
☐ d. 1832

149 Which of these is not a public health measure taken by the Liberal Government of 1906–14?

☐ a. The Old Age Pensions Act
☐ b. The National Insurance Act
☐ c. The provision of free school meals to the poorest children
☐ d. The foundation of the NHS

150 In which year did the new Labour Government introduce the National Health Service?

☐ a. 1939
☐ b. 1945
☐ c. 1929
☐ d. 1948

Geography
uestions

Tectonic processes

1 What is a volcano made up of lava and ash called?

- ☐ a. Active
- ☐ b. Magma
- ☐ c. Composition
- ☐ d. Composite

2 There are destructive, constructive, and conservative plate margins. What is a conservative margin?

- ☐ a. One plate is forced under another
- ☐ b. The plates move alongside each other, often causing earthquakes
- ☐ c. Plates pulling apart
- ☐ d. The plates move alongside each other, often causing volcanoes

3 The Earth's crust is divided into plates. What causes their movement?

- ☐ a. Constructive currents
- ☐ b. Convectional currents in the core
- ☐ c. Convectional rain
- ☐ d. Convection currents in the mantle

4 Volcanoes can be described as active, dormant, or extinct. What is a dormant volcano?

- ☐ a. A volcano that has not erupted for many years
- ☐ b. A volcano that will not erupt again
- ☐ c. A volcano that is erupting at the moment
- ☐ d. A volcano that is expected to erupt soon

5 Which is the best list of emergency supplies required in the event of an earthquake?

- ☐ a. First aid kit, radio, batteries, blankets, tins of food, bottled water
- ☐ b. Suitcase, first aid kit, electric lamp
- ☐ c. Radio, iron, plasters, barbeque
- ☐ d. Tool kit, television, batteries, food, torch

6 Which area is likely to be worst affected by an earthquake of magnitude 7?

- ☐ a. A rural area in a More Economically Developed Country (MEDC)

☐ b. An urban area in a Less
   Economically Developed
   Country (LEDC)
☐ c. An urban area in a More
   Economically Developed
   Country (MEDC)
☐ d. A rural area in a Less
   Economically Developed
   Country (LEDC)

7 The epicentre and focus are words used to describe the location of an earthquake. What is the epicentre?

☐ a. The position of the seismometer
☐ b. The point directly beneath the focus
☐ c. The point at the surface immediately above the focus
☐ d. The origin of the earthquake

8 The Himalayas are still being created. What has caused their formation?

☐ a. Indo-Australian and Antarctican plates pulling apart
☐ b. Nazca and Eurasian plates pushing together
☐ c. Eurasian and African plates pulling apart
☐ d. The Eurasian and Indo-Australian plates moving together

9 Which plates are pulling apart to create the mid-Atlantic ridge?

☐ a. South American and Nazca
☐ b. North American and Eurasian
☐ c. Eurasian and African
☐ d. North American and South American

10 The Richter scale measures the magnitude of an earthquake. How many times more powerful is 7 than 6 on the Richter scale?

☐ a. 7
☐ b. 1
☐ c. 10
☐ d. 6

11 The 'Ring of Fire' is used to describe a string of volcanoes around which ocean?

☐ a. Indian
☐ b. Atlantic
☐ c. Pacific
☐ d. Southern

12 All the rock that makes up the Earth's crust can be put into which three categories?

☐ a. Sedimentary, basalt, granite
☐ b. Igneous, sedimentary, metamorphic
☐ c. Igneous, sandstone, metamorphic
☐ d. Granite, basalt, lava

13 What causes a subduction zone?

☐ a. Plates pulling apart
☐ b. Sedimentary rock being pushed upwards
☐ c. One plate pushing underneath another
☐ d. One plate sliding past another

14 What is a tsunami?

☐ a. A hurricane
☐ b. A fish
☐ c. A tidal wave
☐ d. A volcano

15 Which of the following are all features of a volcano?

☐ a. Ventricle, crater, magma chamber

☐ b. Vent, crater, magma chamber, parasitic cone

☐ c. Magnetic chamber, vent, pyroclastic flow

☐ d. Parasitic cone, vent, delta

16 Monitoring, good planning, education, emergency supplies, and building design are all prerequisites for what?

☐ a. Reducing the impact of mud-slides

☐ b. Reducing the impact of drought

☐ c. Reducing the impact of earthquakes and volcanoes

☐ d. Reducing the impact of rising sea level

17 Which US state contains the San Andreas Fault, which causes devastating earthquakes?

☐ a. Texas

☐ b. Hawaii

☐ c. Washington

☐ d. California

Coasts

18 Which of the following features have not been created as a result of coastal deposition?

☐ a. Tombolos

☐ b. Spits

☐ c. Groynes

☐ d. Bars

19 Many coastal features owe their formation to the variation in rock resistance. Which of the following do not fall into this category?

☐ a. Headlands

☐ b. Caves

☐ c. Spits

☐ d. Bays

20 Which of the following is not a coastal landform?

☐ a. Spit

☐ b. Headland

☐ c. Wave-cut platform

☐ d. Truncated spur

21 The energy of a wave is to a certain extent dependent on the fetch. What is this?

☐ a. The height and length of a wave

☐ b. The speed of a wave

☐ c. The distance a particle is moved by the action of longshore drift

☐ d. The distance of open sea over which the wind has blown

22 What is longshore drift?

☐ a. The washing up of debris on the beach

☐ b. The trapping of sediment on the beach by groynes

☐ c. The erosion of cliffs by the waves

☐ d. The movement of beach material along a coastline by waves

23 Which of the following will not increase the movement of material along a beach?

☐ a. Waves reaching the beach at a right angle
☐ b. Shallow beach gradient
☐ c. Powerful wave action
☐ d. Small particle size

24 What is formed when two caves on either side of a headland join?

☐ a. A large cave
☐ b. A stack
☐ c. A natural arch
☐ d. A bay

25 Defending properties and land against the sea is vital in some locations. Which of the following would be most helpful?

☐ a. Sea wall, revetments, importing sand
☐ b. Managed retreat, evacuation procedures being put into place
☐ c. Planting trees, selling property, managed retreat
☐ d. Warning sirens, sand bags, the coastguard

26 Backwash is the retreating water of the waves washing material towards the sea and at right angles to the beach. What word means the forward movement of the waves, moving the material diagonally up the beach?

☐ a. Erosion
☐ b. Swish
☐ c. Swash
☐ d. Longshore drift

Drainage basins and rivers

27 As air cools, water vapour is transformed into water droplets, which form clouds. Which part of the Hydrological Cycle does this refer to?

☐ a. Evapotranspiration
☐ b. Evaporation
☐ c. Condensation
☐ d. Coagulation

28 There are three main processes of river erosion: corrasion, hydraulic action, and corrosion. What is corrasion?

☐ a. Wearing away of the bed and banks of a river through the action of the water itself
☐ b. Wearing away of the bed and banks of a river through the impacting of the river's load against them
☐ c. Wearing away of the load of a river by the action of water
☐ d. Wearing away of the load of a river through rock and stones colliding

29 How can an upper valley cross-profile usually be described?

☐ a. A wide floor and steep sides
☐ b. A narrow floor and gently sloping sides
☐ c. A wide floor and gently sloping sides
☐ d. A narrow floor and steep sides

30 What will create the most deposition along a river profile?

- [ ] a. When the gradient is high and the volume is low
- [ ] b. When the gradient and volume are high
- [ ] c. When the gradient and volume are low
- [ ] d. When the gradient is high and the river is straight

31 A body of water is heated by the sun and water vapour rises into the atmosphere. What is this called?

- [ ] a. Water cycle
- [ ] b. Evaporation
- [ ] c. Evapotranspiration
- [ ] d. Condensation

32 How will straightening and concreting a river channel affect the likelihood of that river flooding?

- [ ] a. Reduce it
- [ ] b. Increase it
- [ ] c. Keep it the same
- [ ] d. Make it worse in summer but not in winter

33 How can hydraulic action be described?

- [ ] a. Water dissolving the material
- [ ] b. The wearing away of the river bed by the bedload
- [ ] c. The force of water wearing away rock
- [ ] d. Sediment particles knocking against each other and becoming smaller

34 How does water move horizontally through the hydrological cycle?

- [ ] a. Surface run-off and infiltration
- [ ] b. Percolation and through flow
- [ ] c. Stem flow and infiltration
- [ ] d. Through flow and ground water flow

35 The hydrological cycle is dependent on which processes?

- [ ] a. Evaporation and conversation
- [ ] b. Evaporation and condensation
- [ ] c. Evacuation and condensation
- [ ] d. Evaporation and convection

36 How does water move vertically through the ground?

- [ ] a. Ground water flow and interception
- [ ] b. Surface run-off and through flow
- [ ] c. Infiltration and percolation
- [ ] d. Interception and surface run-off

37 Along the river profile, where is lateral erosion most common?

- [ ] a. Upper stages
- [ ] b. Lower stages
- [ ] c. Head of the valley
- [ ] d. Middle stage

38 What is the load of the river most likely to be like in the upper reaches of a river?

- [ ] a. Small and rounded
- [ ] b. Large and rounded
- [ ] c. Large and angular
- [ ] d. Small and angular

39 Which statement most accurately describes a meander?

- [ ] a. There is deposition on the outside of the bend where the river is faster
- [ ] b. Erosion is greatest on the inside of the bend where the river is faster
- [ ] c. The current is fastest on the outside of the bend where the river is deeper
- [ ] d. The current is slower on the outside of the bend where the river is deeper

40 River discharge is the amount of water in a river channel. How can this be expressed in the form of a simple equation?

- [ ] a. Discharge = Depth × Cross-sectional Area
- [ ] b. Discharge = Width × Cross-sectional Area
- [ ] c. Discharge = Volume × Cross-sectional Area
- [ ] d. Discharge = Volume × Wetted Perimeter

41 The methods of moving material down a river vary according to sediment size. Which list gives you the method of transportation of particle size from smallest to largest?

- [ ] a. Solution, suspension, saltation, traction
- [ ] b. Saltation, solution, traction, suspension
- [ ] c. Solution, saltation, solution, traction
- [ ] d. Traction, saltation, suspension, solution

42 When will the velocity of a river be at its greatest?

- [ ] a. When the discharge and gradient are low
- [ ] b. When the discharge is low but the gradient is high
- [ ] c. When the discharge is high but the gradient is low
- [ ] d. When the discharge and gradient are the greatest

43 What is a tributary?

- [ ] a. The point where two rivers join
- [ ] b. The origin of a river
- [ ] c. The area drained by a river
- [ ] d. A smaller river joining a larger river

44 In what ways can water be stored within the hydrological cycle?

- [ ] a. Clouds and taps
- [ ] b. Swimming pools, clouds, and aqueous solutions
- [ ] c. Evaporation and lakes
- [ ] d. Rivers, lakes, and aquifers

45 What is high ground separating two drainage basins called?

- [ ] a. Watershed
- [ ] b. Catchment area
- [ ] c. Confluence
- [ ] d. Mouth

Glaciation

46 What are the two main processes of ice erosion?

- [ ] a. Abrasion and plucking
- [ ] b. Abrasion and sanding

☐ c. Biological weathering and freeze-thaw
☐ d. Corrosion and chemical weathering

47 What is 'a long winding ridge of sand and gravel material'?

☐ a. An esker
☐ b. A ground moraine
☐ c. A drumlin
☐ d. An erratic

48 Which of the following are all glacial features?

☐ a. Interlocking spurs, arete, V-shaped valley
☐ b. Hanging valley, tarn, tombolo
☐ c. U-shaped valley, ox-bow lakes
☐ d. Hanging valley, corrie, truncated spurs

49 What are terminal moraines?

☐ a. Rocks that have been moved and left behind by a retreating glacier
☐ b. Eroded drumlins
☐ c. A deep rounded hollow formed by a glacier
☐ d. Ridges of material that mark the past boundary between a glacial and a periglacial area

Weathering and rocks

50 What is biological weathering?

☐ a. The action of plant roots growing through rocks and loosening fragments
☐ b. Water freezing and thawing in cracks in the rock
☐ c. The action of washing powder on clothes

☐ d. The expansion and contraction of rocks due to extremes of heat

51 Rocks are broken down and worn away through exposure to such things as the atmosphere and animals. What is the difference between erosion and weathering?

☐ a. Weathering does not transport the broken-down rocks to another location
☐ b. Erosion is the effect of acid rain on rocks
☐ c. Erosion does not transport the broken-down rocks to another location
☐ d. There is no difference

52 What is exfoliation (onion skin weathering)?

☐ a. The 'peeling off' of layers of rock due to extremes of heat and cold
☐ b. The effect of the weather on skin
☐ c. The loss of leaves from trees
☐ d. The weathering of rock due to chemical action

53 From what are clints, grykes, stalagmites, and stalactites formed?

☐ a. Basalt
☐ b. Limestone
☐ c. Granite
☐ d. Sandstone

54 Which rocks are formed by heat or pressure and as a result are harder and more compact?

☐ a. Sedimentary
☐ b. Igneous
☐ c. Metamorphic
☐ d. Lava

55 Which rocks are formed in the sea?

☐ a. Basalt
☐ b. Sedimentary
☐ c. Metamorphic
☐ d. Igneous

56 Which of the following are sedimentary rocks?

☐ a. Marble, granite
☐ b. Limestone, sandstone
☐ c. Lava, slate
☐ d. Slate, basalt

57 What are stalactites?

☐ a. A column of calcium deposits from floor to ceiling
☐ b. Calcium deposits that grow vertically from the ground
☐ c. A hole in the roof of a cave
☐ d. Calcium deposits that hang down from the roof of a cave

58 A bed of hard rock surrounded by softer rock, allowing undercutting to occur, is most likely to create which features?

☐ a. Meanders and ox-bow lakes
☐ b. Interlocking spurs and valley
☐ c. River estuary and meanders
☐ d. A waterfall and gorge

Weather and climate

59 What are the summers and winters like in the savannah areas located between the Tropic of Cancer and the Tropic of Capricorn?

☐ a. Wet summers and dry winters
☐ b. Drought conditions throughout the year

☐ c. Dry summers and wet winters
☐ d. Rainfall spread out throughout the year

60 Which term best describes fog that has been caused by warm, moist air blowing over a cooler surface so that the lower air temperature is reduced?

☐ a. Smog
☐ b. Radiation
☐ c. Advection
☐ d. Frontal

61 Anticyclones are associated with which kind of weather?

☐ a. Dry hot conditions in summer but cold rainy days in winter
☐ b. Dry hot conditions in summer, sunny but cold days in winter
☐ c. Mild wet days in summer and cold dry days in winter
☐ d. Mild wet days in summer and mild wet days in winter

62 In northern latitudes, high pressure is called an anticyclone. Which of the following best describes anticyclones?

☐ a. A mass of ascending air that discourages rain
☐ b. A mass of ascending air that encourages rain
☐ c. A mass of descending air that discourages rain
☐ d. A mass of descending air that encourages rain

63 Which of the following is the most dominant feature of the UK's weather?

☐ a. Anticyclones
☐ b. Relief rainfall

☐ c. Tornados
☐ d. Depressions

64 As a depression passes overhead, what sequence of weather would you expect?

☐ a. Drizzle and cold air followed by warmer dry air then heavier but shorter lived rainfall and colder air
☐ b. Drizzle and warm air followed by cooler but drier air then finally a long period of heavier rainfall and warmer temperatures
☐ c. Drizzle and cold air followed by heavier but short-lived rainfall and an increase in temperature then a dry spell
☐ d. Heavy but short-lived rainfall and cool air followed by warmer air and showers and finally drizzle and a return to the cooler air

65 There are three types of rainfall: frontal, convectional, and relief. What causes frontal rain?

☐ a. Air rising over a mountain causing the water vapour to cool and condense
☐ b. Warm air being undercut by colder air in a low-pressure system
☐ c. Cold air being undercut by warm air in a high-pressure system
☐ d. Warmer air rising through colder air

66 Which of the following statements is not true for hurricanes?

☐ a. They form over tropical seas
☐ b. They form when the temperature is higher than 26°C
☐ c. They occur in late summer or early autumn
☐ d. They originate exactly 23.5° north and south of the equator

67 Hurricanes are violent storms that occur in the Atlantic, but what is the name for a violent storm of the Pacific?

☐ a. Typhoon
☐ b. Tornado
☐ c. Tsunami
☐ d. Water spout

68 What is the line on a map that joins places having the same amount of rainfall?

☐ a. Isohyet
☐ b. Isostatic
☐ c. Isobar
☐ d. Isotherm

69 Barometers measure pressure in what?

☐ a. Isobars
☐ b. Millibars
☐ c. Isohyets
☐ d. Newtons

70 If the prevailing winds approach from the west and then rise over a mountain range that runs north to south, where would the rain shadow area be?

☐ a. To the west of the mountains
☐ b. On top of the mountains
☐ c. To the east of the mountains
☐ d. To the south of the mountains

71 The UK receives which types of rainfall?

☐ a. Convectional, frontal, and relief
☐ b. Convectional and relief
☐ c. Convectional and frontal
☐ d. Relief and frontal

72 As latitude increases what happens to temperature?

☐ a. It decreases and the temperature range also decreases
☐ b. It decreases but the temperature range increases
☐ c. It increases but the temperature range decreases
☐ d. It increases and the temperature range also increases

73 Locations near the coast generally have a smaller temperature range than those inland. Why is this?

☐ a. They get more rain
☐ b. Land heats up and cools down more slowly than the sea
☐ c. Land heats up and cools down more quickly than the sea
☐ d. They are always at a lower altitude

74 What are prevailing westerlies in Britain?

☐ a. Hurricanes
☐ b. Cyclones
☐ c. Winds
☐ d. Tides

75 When does it usually rain in the tropical rainforest regions?

☐ a. Summer
☐ b. Every afternoon
☐ c. Every morning
☐ d. Winter

76 What is global warming?

☐ a. The heating of the Earth's core
☐ b. The destruction of the ozone layer
☐ c. The rise of the Earth's sea level
☐ d. The gradual increase in the Earth's temperature

Ecosystems

77 Why are there so few species in coniferous forests?

☐ a. Falling needles create an alkali layer on the soil that many other plants cannot tolerate
☐ b. Falling needles create an acid layer on the soil that many other plants cannot tolerate
☐ c. The trees grow close together so little light reaches the ground
☐ d. The needles smother other small plants that may grow

78 People affect ecosystems in many ways – deforestation is one. There are many reasons why deforestation might be carried out, including the need for timber and to use the land for farming or urban development. Which of the following is the least likely reason for deforestation?

☐ a. For mineral extraction
☐ b. To help reduce flooding
☐ c. To develop hydroelectric power
☐ d. To build roads

79 Long roots and small, thorny leaves, swollen stems, and a thick waxy skin are all features of plants indigenous to which environment?

☐ a. Tundra
☐ b. Rainforests
☐ c. Deserts
☐ d. Tropical grassland

80 What are the major characteristics of vegetation in hot deserts?

☐ a. Thin skinned with shallow roots
☐ b. Plants that blossom and complete their life cycle in a few weeks
☐ c. Thin skinned with deep roots
☐ d. Large smooth leaves

81 How can the undergrowth in a tropical rainforest best be described?

☐ a. Non-existent
☐ b. Dense
☐ c. Lush
☐ d. Sparse

82 Thick and waxy drip-tip leaves, along with buttress roots, are adaptation plants that have evolved to survive in which environment?

☐ a. Tropical grassland
☐ b. Savannah
☐ c. Tropical rainforest
☐ d. Deserts

83 Tropical grassland will not be found at which of the following locations?

☐ a. Southern Europe
☐ b. Australia
☐ c. Central America
☐ d. South America

84 For plants to survive in the far northern latitudes they have had to develop a number of features. These enable them to overcome the permafrost, short growing season, low rainfall, and strong winds. What are these features?

☐ a. Shallow roots, small leaves, and small size
☐ b. Shallow roots, small leaves, and large size
☐ c. Deep root systems, small leaves, and small size
☐ d. Deep roots, large leaves, and large size

85 Coniferous forests are more usually associated with what kind of soil?

☐ a. Chernozems
☐ b. Salty
☐ c. Brown earths
☐ d. Podsols

86 There are five main components of soils. These include minerals, organisms, organic matter, water, and what else?

☐ a. Air
☐ b. Roots
☐ c. Mud
☐ d. Worms

Population distribution and change

87 How can the relationship between birth rate and death rate be described in Stage 4 of the Demographic Transition Model?

☐ a. Death rates and birth rates are high

b. Birth rates are greater than death rates

c. Death rates are greater than birth rates

d. Birth rates and death rates are low

88 In 1991 there were 11,741 under 16s, 10,598 people of pensionable age, and 35,469 people of working age. For every 100 people of working age, how many were dependent on them?

a. 7

b. 302

c. 63

d. 0.63

89 What is an emigrant?

a. A person who moves into an urban area from a rural area

b. Someone who leaves a particular country

c. Someone who moves into a particular country

d. Someone who moves into a country illegally

90 Which country famously imposed a 'One Child Only Policy'?

a. India

b. China

c. France

d. Japan

91 Which of the following statements is not true for a Less Economically Developed Country (LEDC)?

a. It has a relatively high infant mortality

b. It has a high number of young dependants

c. It has a relatively low life expectancy

d. It has a relatively high number of elderly dependants

92 What is population density?

a. The number of people

b. The area of a country

c. The number of people per unit area

d. The number of people × area

93 There were approximately 5,734 million people worldwide in 1995. Currently it is thought there will be how many millions by 2025?

a. 120,000

b. 8,200

c. 4,500

d. 6,000

94 Which of the following are factors that affect population density across the globe?

a. Building materials, house prices, and job availability

b. Volcanoes, hurricanes, and earthquakes

c. Wild animals, political reasons, and family

d. Climate, soil fertility, and relief

95 To what does the term population explosion refer?

a. The fall in population totals due to bubonic plague in 1665

b. The rapid increase in world population totals during the first millennium

c. The rapid increase in world population during the 20th century

☐ d. The high death rate in Stage 1 of the Demographic Transition Model

96 What does a population pyramid with concave sides indicate?

☐ a. A high death rate
☐ b. A low death rate
☐ c. A high birth rate
☐ d. A low birth rate

97 What is underpopulation?

☐ a. Where there is a balance between resources and the number of people
☐ b. Where there are many houses left empty in a rural settlement
☐ c. Where there are too few people to make the most of the resources available
☐ d. Where there are more people than available resources are able to support to an adequate standard of living

98 Which group of people are most likely to indulge in counter-urbanization?

☐ a. Families in a More Economically Developed Country (MEDC)
☐ b. Retired people in a Less Economically Developed Country (LEDC)
☐ c. Young single people in a More Economically Developed Country (MEDC)
☐ d. Young single people in a Less Economically Developed Country (LEDC)

Settlements

99 In which country are you likely to find game parks?

☐ a. USA
☐ b. Brazil
☐ c. Scotland
☐ d. Kenya

100 Which of the following is not a national park?

☐ a. The Pennines
☐ b. Pembroke Coast
☐ c. The Lake District
☐ d. Brecon Beacons

101 In which of these locations is a major settlement most likely to develop?

☐ a. Near mineral resources
☐ b. On an area of chalk upland
☐ c. On a pass through the mountains
☐ d. At a crossing point on a major river

102 Urban models attempt to simplify the development of urban areas. Where does the Concentric Zone Model state where the most desirable houses of a city will be?

☐ a. In a sector radiating from the centre
☐ b. On the edge
☐ c. In the villages
☐ d. In the centre

103 A conurbation is a very large urban area formed by the joining together of several separate expanding towns and/or cities. Which of the following is not a conurbation?

☐ a. London
☐ b. Manchester
☐ c. Southampton
☐ d. Birmingham

104 What is greenbelt?

☐ a. An area where all planning restrictions have been lifted
☐ b. An area around an urban area where planning controls limit development
☐ c. An area set aside for industry
☐ d. An area of forest near a city

105 The number and type of services vary from settlement to settlement and some settlements will be able to provide high order goods. Which of the following is an example of a high order good?

☐ a. Sweets
☐ b. Loaf of bread
☐ c. Fridge
☐ d. Newspaper

106 Settlement hierarchy ranks settlements according to their size and number. Which list most accurately describes this?

☐ a. Conurbation, city, town, village, hamlet, isolated house
☐ b. City, conurbation, town, village, hamlet, isolated house
☐ c. Conurbation, city, town, hamlet, village, isolated house
☐ d. City, conurbation, town, hamlet, village, isolated house

107 Which is not a term that could be used to describe a shanty town?

☐ a. A favela
☐ b. A conurbation

☐ c. A bustee
☐ d. An unplanned squatter settlement

108 What does sphere of influence mean?

☐ a. The limits of a particular settlement
☐ b. An area outside the urban environment where building is restricted
☐ c. The number of people required to make a service viable
☐ d. The area served by a particular settlement or service

109 Increased urbanization has led to many problems in cities in More Economically Developed Countries (MEDCs) and Less Economically Developed Countries (LEDCs). What best describes some of the major problems in an LEDC city?

☐ a. Vandalism and graffiti caused by unemployed youths with nothing better to do
☐ b. Traditional manufacturing businesses closing down near the city centres, leaving empty derelict buildings
☐ c. High pollution levels as a result of increased traffic caused by more people now commuting to work from the outlying areas and increased property prices
☐ d. Overcrowding, causing pressure on the land, and the building of squatter settlements with few amenities, which often creates health risks

110 Settlements such as Blackpool and Margate could be said to have what main function?

- ☐ a. As administrative centres
- ☐ b. As ports
- ☐ c. As resorts
- ☐ d. As industrial centres

111 Urbanization has created many Millionaire Cities around the world. Which is the world's largest city?

- ☐ a. New York
- ☐ b. Mexico City
- ☐ c. London
- ☐ d. São Paulo

112 Which list most accurately shows how people benefit from living in volcanic zones?

- ☐ a. Reduced house prices, fertile soil, more rainfall
- ☐ b. Hot springs, fertile soils, building materials, warmer climate
- ☐ c. Fertile soils, valuable minerals, geothermal power, tourism
- ☐ d. Warmer climate, geothermal power, cultural beliefs

Economic activity

113 Traditional manufacturing areas in the UK were largely based around what?

- ☐ a. London
- ☐ b. Mountains
- ☐ c. Oil fields
- ☐ d. Coal fields

114 What are 'eco-tourists'?

- ☐ a. Relatively small-scale groups of tourists who explore the wildlife and countryside, sampling the local culture but also respecting and attempting to maintain it
- ☐ b. Groups of people who pay to go on trips to 'clean up the environment'
- ☐ c. Small groups of tourists who visit ecologically sensitive environments
- ☐ d. Groups of people who travel the world protesting against tourism in Less Economically Developed Countries (LEDCs)

115 What is a 'honey pot'?

- ☐ a. A café area within a national park
- ☐ b. An area inhabited by bears
- ☐ c. A cave system in a limestone environment
- ☐ d. A focus point for tourists

116 If the raw materials used by a factory are heavy and bulky and a great deal of waste is generated in production, where is the industry likely to be located?

- ☐ a. Near the raw materials
- ☐ b. Near the labour supply
- ☐ c. Half-way between the raw materials and the market
- ☐ d. Near to the market

117 Which of the following would not help to account for the growth in the leisure industry in recent years?

- ☐ a. Flexible working hours
- ☐ b. Better pay

☐ c. More holidays and free time
☐ d. People are more lazy

118 What are the advantages to a Less Economically Developed Country (LEDC) if a multinational locates in that country?

☐ a. The products are largely made for export and most of the profit is taken out of the host country
☐ b. The host country becomes dependent on the employment and often little regard is taken of the environment
☐ c. The jobs are largely poorly paid and management positions are usually given to foreign nationals
☐ d. It provides jobs and investment and increases international trade

119 What are NICs?

☐ a. Near Indonesian Countries
☐ b. Newly Industrialized Company
☐ c. Nearly Industrialized Countries
☐ d. Newly Industrialized Countries

120 A farmer works in which category of industry?

☐ a. Secondary
☐ b. Tertiary
☐ c. Quaternary
☐ d. Primary

121 Which of the following is a renewable resource?

☐ a. Coal
☐ b. Water
☐ c. Oil
☐ d. Gas

122 Where are science parks least likely to be located?

☐ a. Near similar industries
☐ b. Near universities
☐ c. In the central business district
☐ d. On the outskirts of towns and cities

123 What is a tertiary industry?

☐ a. It is a service – nothing is actually made
☐ b. It is where raw materials are extracted from the earth and not processed in any way
☐ c. It is where new research is undertaken in the fields of information technology and computing
☐ d. It is where a raw material is processed and transformed into another product

124 How can encouraging tourism help Less Economically Developed Countries (LEDCs)?

☐ a. It creates more pollution
☐ b. It makes people more aware that they exist
☐ c. Jobs are created and the money made can be invested locally
☐ d. Much of the money made from the tourism goes out of the country

125 Which of the following would not be a realistic solution to traffic problems in an urban area in a More Economically Developed Country (MEDC)?

☐ a. Pedestrianized residential areas
☐ b. Improved public transport

☐ c. Pedestrianized city centres
☐ d. Cycle routes

126 What is a CBD?

☐ a. Central Busy District
☐ b. Concentric Business District
☐ c. Cities Business District
☐ d. Central Business District

127 Which of the following would not be a commercial farm?

☐ a. Factory farm
☐ b. Slash and burn
☐ c. Plantation
☐ d. Ranch

128 What does CAP stand for?

☐ a. Central Area Parking
☐ b. Common Agricultural Policy
☐ c. Common Awareness Politics
☐ d. Capital Awareness Policy

129 Many farmers are now 'diversifying'. What does this mean?

☐ a. Buying extra land to enlarge their existing farm and make it more profitable
☐ b. Developing business activities in addition to their traditional ones
☐ c. Employing fewer people and instead using more machinery in order to improve efficiency
☐ d. Enlarging the size of their fields to make it easier to use large pieces of machinery and increase the area of land used

130 Which of the following is likely to be an intensive farm?

☐ a. Wheat cultivation in Canada
☐ b. Nomadic herders

☐ c. Sheep farm
☐ d. Market garden

131 The European Union (EU) has imposed many initiatives on farmers. One of these was the introduction of milk quotas. What problems did this cause?

☐ a. Other farmers were resentful of the financial gains
☐ b. It created a milk surplus or 'lake'
☐ c. There were none; it worked very well to link supply and demand
☐ d. Initially much milk was wasted and no allowance was made for diversification of the farms

132 What is a pastoral farm?

☐ a. One that specializes in growing trees
☐ b. One that specializes in growing crops
☐ c. One that specializes in rearing animals
☐ d. One where just enough food is grown for the farmer and the farmer's family

133 Plantations are an important type of agriculture in Less Economically Developed Countries (LEDCs). They are large estates often owned by multinationals or other large land owners. What disadvantages do they hold for the host country?

☐ a. They create a reliance on a single crop and the jobs are usually poorly paid
☐ b. It is difficult to find workers for all the openings created

- [ ] c. They create an overabundance of a particular crop which 'floods the market' in the host country
- [ ] d. Many of the local people become wealthy, which leads to ill feeling

134 Why did the European Union introduce 'Set-Aside'?

- [ ] a. To reduce the over-cultivation of cereals
- [ ] b. Because they thought that many farmers were over worked
- [ ] c. To reduce the amount of oil seed rape grown
- [ ] d. To create more 'green areas' in the countryside

135 The 'Green Revolution' is an expression given to what?

- [ ] a. The rapid and successful rise to positions of influence of the Green Party in the UK and many other European countries in the 1990s
- [ ] b. The development of a more environmentally aware society in the 1980s and 1990s
- [ ] c. The subsidies given to farmers to plant new areas of forest and hedgerows in the 1990s
- [ ] d. The development of new higher yielding and more disease resistant varieties of crops for many Less Economically Developed Countries (LEDCs) in the 1960s

Development

136 Aid is one way by which countries may help one another. What is 'bilateral aid'?

- [ ] a. Aid that is just given once and with no other links made
- [ ] b. Aid given through an agency, usually the World Bank, which then distributes the aid
- [ ] c. Aid given through charities or the fund-raising activities of bodies such as *Blue Peter*
- [ ] d. Aid given directly by one government to another

137 The colonial history of a country often can help to explain why it has been slow in developing. Give an example of a country that was a British colony.

- [ ] a. Japan
- [ ] b. China
- [ ] c. France
- [ ] d. India

138 The richer countries are mostly in the northern hemisphere. What are the two main exceptions to this?

- [ ] a. Ethiopia and Chad
- [ ] b. The United States of America (USA) and Canada
- [ ] c. Brazil and Peru
- [ ] d. Australia and New Zealand

139 Approximately what percentage of the world population live in the More Economically Developed Countries (MEDCs)?

- [ ] a. 20%
- [ ] b. 45%

☐ c. 80%
☐ d. 50%

140 Which of the following is not true for More Economically Developed Countries (MEDCs)?

☐ a. The Gross National Product (GNP) is relatively high
☐ b. The population structure is in Stage 4 of the Demographic Transition Model
☐ c. Primary industries dominate
☐ d. A small percentage of the population works in the primary sector

141 Environmental conditions have traditionally hindered development in some Less Economically Developed Countries (LEDCs). Which of the following does not fall into this category?

☐ a. Extreme climate
☐ b. Pests
☐ c. Natural hazards
☐ d. Pollution

142 The Gross Domestic Product (GDP) per capita refers to what?

☐ a. The total value of goods and services produced in a year divided by the population
☐ b. The average cost of houses for the population
☐ c. The total earnings of the population in a year divided by the number of people
☐ d. The political party that most people vote for in that country

143 There are many ways of helping to measure development. Life expectancy, infant mortality, and number of people per doctor are only three of them. What does infant mortality mean?

☐ a. For every thousand live births it is the number of children who die under the age of 16 years
☐ b. The number of children who die under the age of five years from every thousand live births
☐ c. The number of babies who survive beyond one year from every thousand live births
☐ d. For every thousand live births it is the number of babies who die aged under one year

144 When aid is given in the form of development projects often it is the smaller scale projects that are most likely to succeed. Why?

☐ a. They get more media attention
☐ b. Because it is small scale, really up-to-date technology can be brought in
☐ c. They focus on specific improvements or needs of a small area and usually involve training for the local people
☐ d. They can be imposed on a population without the outside organization having to become involved

145 A way of improving the standard of living and quality of life of people, without wasting resources or harming the environment, is called what?

☐ a. Aid
☐ b. Sustainable development

☐ c. Eco-tourism
☐ d. Common Agricultural Policy

Environmental issues

146 What is geothermal power?

☐ a. The use of the power of the wind
☐ b. The use of the power of water
☐ c. The use of heat energy from beneath the ground
☐ d. The use of heat energy from the sun

147 What causes acid rain?

☐ a. The hole in the ozone layer
☐ b. Moist air masses rising over mountains
☐ c. Chemical works
☐ d. The burning of fossil fuels

148 What is put into lakes affected by acid rain to restore them?

☐ a. Lime
☐ b. Lemon juice
☐ c. Fertilizer
☐ d. Vinegar

149 The various demands made of glaciated highland often lead to conflicts between different groups. Which of the following most accurately covers the groups concerned?

☐ a. National parks, shop owners, the Forestry Commission, urban planners
☐ b. Shop owners, conservationists, doctors

☐ c. Conservationists, farmers, shop owners
☐ d. National parks, farmers, tourists, conservationists

150 For what are glaciated highlands not likely to be used?

☐ a. For sheep farming
☐ b. For tourism
☐ c. For hydroelectric power
☐ d. For arable farming

Music
Questions

Music Questions

Notation

1 The G clef is more commonly known as which clef?

☐ a. Alto
☐ b. Bass
☐ c. Treble
☐ d. Tenor

2 If a piece of music says pianissimo, how should it be played?

☐ a. Loudly
☐ b. Softly
☐ c. Very softly
☐ d. Quickly

3 Which of these words would tell you to play a note or chord with a sudden emphasis?

☐ a. Staccato
☐ b. Sforzando
☐ c. Crescendo
☐ d. Forte

4 Which form of notation was originally used in medieval plainchant, reappeared in the 1850s, and records visual traces of recorded sounds?

☐ a. Score
☐ b. Graph notation
☐ c. Clefs
☐ d. Stave

5 On a musical score, which instruments are normally grouped together at the bottom of the system?

☐ a. Percussion
☐ b. Strings
☐ c. Brass
☐ d. Woodwind

6 On a musical score, the individual staves are grouped together on the left-hand side. What is this group of staves called?

☐ a. Grouped stave
☐ b. System
☐ c. Suite
☐ d. Score

Genres, styles, and traditions

7 Which culture's music is based on a strong percussive beat that is emphasized by wind and string players as well as by clapping and drummers?

a. African
b. Indian
c. German
d. US

a. Chopin
b. Bizet
c. Charpentier
d. Berlioz

8 The music of which country consists mainly of highly stylized and descriptive operas based on the pentatonic scale?

a. USA
b. China
c. West Indies
d. Africa

12 What is the name for a piece of music, usually with three movements, composed for a solo instrument and orchestra?

a. Overture
b. Symphony
c. Eisteddford
d. Concerto

9 Which country's music is usually performed by a 'gamelan' of 30–40 players, with each gamelan using instruments made in the players' own village?

a. France
b. China
c. Australia
d. Indonesia

13 What name is given to a short ceremonial piece, usually written for valveless trumpets and played on the arrival of an important figure?

a. Fugue
b. Fanfare
c. Symphony
d. Cantata

10 Which Austrian composer wrote more then 100 symphonies and pieces of choral music, including oratorios, and was the first master of the string quartet?

a. Diabelli
b. J S Bach
c. Schubert
d. Haydn

14 Which type of piece is in duple time with a strongly marked beat and regular phrasing, and is written for soldiers or a procession?

a. Toccata
b. March
c. Chorale
d. Anthem

11 Which French composer was thought to be the founder of modern orchestration and whose music was inspired by drama and literature?

15 Governments of the early 20th century encouraged composers to make use of traditional folk music in their compositions. What was this known as?

a. Minimalism
b. Nationalism
c. Serialism
d. Romanticism

16 Which of these is a medieval chant, sung in unison with no harmony and no definitely measured rhythm?

- ☐ a. Aria
- ☐ b. Plainsong
- ☐ c. Cantata
- ☐ d. Chorale

17 What is the term for instrumental music that depicts a scene or painting or interprets a story?

- ☐ a. Patronage
- ☐ b. Romanticism
- ☐ c. Opera
- ☐ d. Programme music

18 Which of the following describes the device introduced by Schoenberg, whereby all 12 notes of the chromatic scale are treated equally and used in a sequence that is then repeated in various ways?

- ☐ a. Sequencing
- ☐ b. Serialism
- ☐ c. Romanticism
- ☐ d. Minimalism

19 Which large-scale orchestral work traditionally has four movements, one of which is in sonata form?

- ☐ a. Concerto
- ☐ b. Suite
- ☐ c. Symphony
- ☐ d. Fantasia

20 For which of these instruments would a toccata most likely be written?

- ☐ a. Synthesizer
- ☐ b. Violin
- ☐ c. Harp
- ☐ d. Organ

21 Which dance is in 3/4 time with a strong first beat to each bar?

- ☐ a. Saraband
- ☐ b. Tango
- ☐ c. Ballet
- ☐ d. Waltz

22 Which baroque composer wrote over 400 concertos and is best known for *The Four Seasons*?

- ☐ a. Mozart
- ☐ b. Paganini
- ☐ c. Vivaldi
- ☐ d. Telemann

23 Which 20th-century US composer wrote works with realistic contemporary themes including a renamed modern adaptation of *Romeo and Juliet*?

- ☐ a. Lloyd Weber
- ☐ b. Bernstein
- ☐ c. Schoenberg
- ☐ d. Britten

24 Which Italian composer was a master of Renaissance counterpoint and wrote 105 masses as well as motets and madrigals?

- ☐ a. Dowland
- ☐ b. Tallis
- ☐ c. Palestrina
- ☐ d. Gabrieli

25 Which baroque composer was considered to be the master of counterpoint, was from a well-known family of composers, and whose works included 48 preludes and fugues?

☐ a. J S Bach
☐ b. Scarlatti
☐ c. Pachelbel
☐ d. Corelli

26 Which 20th-century US composer experimented with the prepared piano?

☐ a. Shostakovich
☐ b. Cage
☐ c. Britten
☐ d. Bernstein

27 Which German composer and pianist led the way in emotional musical expression for Romantic composers of the 19th century?

☐ a. Dvorak
☐ b. Debussy
☐ c. Elgar
☐ d. Beethoven

28 Which three-valved soprano brass instrument was developed for military band use?

☐ a. Trombone
☐ b. Cornet
☐ c. Trumpet
☐ d. French horn

29 Which of these was an early four- or five-part secular song performed without accompaniment?

☐ a. Lied
☐ b. Madrigal
☐ c. Aria
☐ d. Oratorio

30 Which style of music developed from operettas and musical comedies of the 19th century and appeals to a wide range of audiences today?

☐ a. Oratorio
☐ b. Ballet
☐ c. Musicals
☐ d. Operas

31 What is the name for an opening piece of an opera or musical?

☐ a. Symphony
☐ b. Overture
☐ c. Intermezzo
☐ d. Finale

32 Which of these is not a standard member of the orchestra?

☐ a. Trombone
☐ b. Saxophone
☐ c. Timpani
☐ d. Cello

33 Which section of the orchestra contains the instruments that can be divided into two subsections – those that are tuned and those of indefinite pitch?

☐ a. Brass
☐ b. Strings
☐ c. Woodwind
☐ d. Percussion

34 Which of these does not form part of the string quartet?

☐ a. First violin
☐ b. Cello
☐ c. Double bass
☐ d. Second violin

35 Miles Davis, Louis Armstrong, and Charlie Parker were all pioneers of which style of music?

- ☐ a. Blues
- ☐ b. Country
- ☐ c. Pop
- ☐ d. Jazz

36 Which style of popular music is played very loudly and relies heavily on the electric guitar?

- ☐ a. Heavy metal
- ☐ b. Reggae
- ☐ c. Rap
- ☐ d. Punk

37 Which type of popular music is based on chanted poetry or rhymes, is accompanied by a strong rhythmic beat, and has African origins?

- ☐ a. Rap
- ☐ b. Bluegrass
- ☐ c. Rock
- ☐ d. Soul

38 Which North American folk music has a natural form, and was first played and sung by African-Americans to portray unhappy or difficult times?

- ☐ a. Country
- ☐ b. Swing
- ☐ c. Jazz
- ☐ d. Blues

39 Which US singer of the mid-1960s was famed for his folk-rock style?

- ☐ a. Bob Dylan
- ☐ b. Stevie Wonder
- ☐ c. Kenny Rogers
- ☐ d. James Brown

40 Which rock group of the 1960s came from Liverpool and was the most successful group in pop history?

- ☐ a. The Who
- ☐ b. The Beach Boys
- ☐ c. The Rolling Stones
- ☐ d. The Beatles

Instruments and musical features

41 What is the term for an accompaniment built on broken chords that was popular in the 18th century?

- ☐ a. Alberti bass
- ☐ b. Basso continuo
- ☐ c. Ground bass
- ☐ d. Ostinato

42 Which of these words would tell you to play a piece of music at a walking pace?

- ☐ a. Vivace
- ☐ b. Moderato
- ☐ c. Largo
- ☐ d. Andante

43 Which of these words would tell you to slow down gradually a piece of music, and would often be found at the end of a piece?

- ☐ a. Accelerando
- ☐ b. Allargando
- ☐ c. Ritardando
- ☐ d. Morendo

44 Which form in music consists of symmetrical halves, the first modulating to the dominant key and the second modulating back to the tonic?

- [ ] a. Ternary
- [ ] b. Binary
- [ ] c. Sonata
- [ ] d. Ritornello

45 What is the term for a contrapuntal piece where a number of parts enter in succession in direct imitation of one another?

- [ ] a. Fugue
- [ ] b. Ritornello
- [ ] c. Sequence
- [ ] d. Ostinato

46 Which woodwind instrument in B flat has the widest range of all modern woodwind instruments?

- [ ] a. Oboe
- [ ] b. Clarinet
- [ ] c. Flute
- [ ] d. Bassoon

47 What is the technique used by male singers to sing notes above their usual range?

- [ ] a. Falsetto
- [ ] b. Chest voice
- [ ] c. Castrato
- [ ] d. Vibrato

48 If a piece of music has pedal markings, which of these instruments would it have been written for?

- [ ] a. Trombone
- [ ] b. Synthesizer
- [ ] c. Cello
- [ ] d. Piano

49 Which instrument's name is derived from the Italian terms for loud and soft?

- [ ] a. Clarinet

- [ ] b. Saxophone
- [ ] c. Violin
- [ ] d. Pianoforte

50 In a four-part vocal score, which voice would you expect to find at the top of the stave?

- [ ] a. Tenor
- [ ] b. Soprano
- [ ] c. Bass
- [ ] d. Alto

51 Which string instrument usually uses the alto clef?

- [ ] a. Viola
- [ ] b. Double bass
- [ ] c. Violin
- [ ] d. Cello

52 Which of these instruments might play pizzicato?

- [ ] a. Oboe
- [ ] b. Piano
- [ ] c. Violin
- [ ] d. Trumpet

53 What is concert pitch?

- [ ] a. The standard pitch, usually A, to which orchestras tune
- [ ] b. The standard pitch, usually C, to which orchestras tune
- [ ] c. The key of the piece that an orchestra is playing
- [ ] d. The term used to describe how high or low a note is

54 Which brass instrument has the lowest tone of any orchestral instrument?

- [ ] a. Tenor horn
- [ ] b. Trombone
- [ ] c. Tuba

☐ d. Cornet

55 Which is the lowest of the male singing voices?

☐ a. Baritone
☐ b. Castrato
☐ c. Bass
☐ d. Tenor

56 Trumpets, trombones, horns, and bugles belong to which family of instruments?

☐ a. Brass
☐ b. Woodwind
☐ c. Strings
☐ d. Percussion

57 Which valved brass instrument, a descendant of the hunting horn, is curved into a circular loop?

☐ a. Tuba
☐ b. Trombone
☐ c. Bugle
☐ d. French horn

58 Which of these musical instruments would not be banged?

☐ a. Tabla
☐ b. Kalimba
☐ c. Bongoes
☐ d. Claves

59 Which of the following instruments is not Indian?

☐ a. Sitar
☐ b. Metallophones
☐ c. Tabla
☐ d. Sarod

60 The viol was a six-stringed musical instrument played with a bow during the Renaissance. How was it held?

☐ a. Cradled in the arm
☐ b. Resting on the leg or knee
☐ c. Under the chin
☐ d. Standing on the ground

61 What has a hollow body, a fingerboard, a bridge, and four catgut strings tuned in fifths?

☐ a. Violin
☐ b. Lyre
☐ c. Classical guitar
☐ d. Harp

62 Which percussion instrument has a name that means 'little drum'?

☐ a. Castanets
☐ b. Glockenspiel
☐ c. Tubular bells
☐ d. Tambourine

63 Basso continuo was a common feature in music of which era?

☐ a. 20th century
☐ b. Romantic
☐ c. Classical
☐ d. Baroque

64 What term describes a repeating figure in the bass, over which different harmonic melodies are played?

☐ a. Ground bass
☐ b. Ostinato
☐ c. Continuo
☐ d. Alberti bass

65 What term describes a persistently repeating melodic or rhythmic figure?

- ☐ a. Ostinato
- ☐ b. Composition
- ☐ c. Sequence
- ☐ d. Continuo

66 What is the term for the numbers that indicate which notes should be played by the continuo player?

- ☐ a. Alberti bass
- ☐ b. Numbered bass
- ☐ c. Ground bass
- ☐ d. Figured bass

67 Which of these is not a section of the sonata form?

- ☐ a. Development
- ☐ b. Exposition
- ☐ c. Recapitulation
- ☐ d. Introduction

68 What is the term for music in 6/8 time?

- ☐ a. Compound duple
- ☐ b. Simple duple
- ☐ c. Simple triple
- ☐ d. Compound triple

69 What term describes the speed of a piece of music, often indicated by a metronome marking?

- ☐ a. Tempo
- ☐ b. Time signature
- ☐ c. Rhythm
- ☐ d. Pace

70 How does a dot to the right of a note affect it?

- ☐ a. Makes it twice its original value
- ☐ b. Means you play it staccato
- ☐ c. Makes it half a beat longer
- ☐ d. Prolongs it by half its original value

71 What is the name of a group of three notes played in the time of two?

- ☐ a. Irregular beat
- ☐ b. Duplet
- ☐ c. Triplet
- ☐ d. Dotted rhythm

72 What is the term for the pattern of beats in a piece of music?

- ☐ a. Metre
- ☐ b. Rhythm
- ☐ c. Time signature
- ☐ d. Tempo

73 When the strong accent is displaced so that it falls on a note that is not normally accented (for example, on the second quaver of a crotchet), what is this known as?

- ☐ a. Suspension
- ☐ b. Downbeat
- ☐ c. Upbeat
- ☐ d. Syncopation

74 What musical sign indicates the metre of a piece of music?

- ☐ a. Clef
- ☐ b. Time signature
- ☐ c. Dynamic
- ☐ d. Key signature

75 What is the term for frequency in music, corresponding to the number of cycles per second?

- ☐ a. Tuning
- ☐ b. Pitch
- ☐ c. Note
- ☐ d. Hertz

76 Which word describes the quality of tone or tone colour of a particular sound?

- ☐ a. Timbre
- ☐ b. Tempo
- ☐ c. Quality
- ☐ d. Acoustics

77 What is the term for music that has no apparent key?

- ☐ a. Diatonic
- ☐ b. Modal
- ☐ c. Dissonant
- ☐ d. Atonal

78 What term could be used to describe contrapuntal music?

- ☐ a. Polyphonic
- ☐ b. Homophonic
- ☐ c. Antiphonic
- ☐ d. Monophonic

79 What is harmony?

- ☐ a. The quality of tone characteristic of a particular instrument or voice
- ☐ b. A distinctive sequence of notes sounded consecutively within an orderly pitch structure such as a scale
- ☐ c. The speed at which a piece should sound
- ☐ d. The combining of notes into chords so that they are heard simultaneously

80 What is the name of a group of three or more notes sounded together?

- ☐ a. Texture
- ☐ b. Scale
- ☐ c. Chord
- ☐ d. Accompaniment

81 In the key of C, what is the bottom (or bass) note of the dominant 7th chord in the first inversion?

- ☐ a. B flat
- ☐ b. G
- ☐ c. C
- ☐ d. B

82 The chords V, VI at the end of a section form which cadence?

- ☐ a. Imperfect
- ☐ b. Plagal
- ☐ c. Interrupted
- ☐ d. Perfect

83 In music, which 12-note scale proceeds by semitones?

- ☐ a. Minor
- ☐ b. Diatonic
- ☐ c. Major
- ☐ d. Chromatic

84 Which key has four sharps in the key signature and no accidentals?

- ☐ a. A major
- ☐ b. E major
- ☐ c. G minor
- ☐ d. F sharp major

85 What is the relative minor key of G major?

- ☐ a. D minor
- ☐ b. C minor
- ☐ c. E minor
- ☐ d. G minor

86 Which scale contains different notes on the way up from the notes on the way down?

- ☐ a. Melodic minor
- ☐ b. Major
- ☐ c. Chromatic
- ☐ d. Harmonic minor

87 Which of the following would tell you to raise a note by one semitone?

- ☐ a. Natural
- ☐ b. Sharp
- ☐ c. Key signature
- ☐ d. Flat

88 What is the term for the effect of our surroundings on the music that we hear?

- ☐ a. Tone
- ☐ b. Acoustics
- ☐ c. Echo
- ☐ d. Harmonics

89 What is the term for music that is played through two speakers?

- ☐ a. Monophonic
- ☐ b. Digital
- ☐ c. Quadraphonic
- ☐ d. Stereophonic

90 Which electronic device can be programmed to reproduce sounds of a musical instrument or the voice?

- ☐ a. Synthesizer
- ☐ b. Tweeter
- ☐ c. Woofer
- ☐ d. Amplifier

Business Studies
Questions

Finance

1 Which of these is not one of the three major financial reports of a company?

- [ ] a. Profit and loss account
- [ ] b. Balance sheet
- [ ] c. Stock account
- [ ] d. Cashflow statement

2 Which of the following is an example of a franchise?

- [ ] a. A charity
- [ ] b. A business that cannot make a profit and decides to sell a part of its product range
- [ ] c. A business that has more than one product
- [ ] d. A business that sells the right to trade under its name to businesses in various locations

3 What can an entrepreneur be defined as?

- [ ] a. Someone who produces a profit
- [ ] b. Someone who develops products of high quality using sophisticated techniques
- [ ] c. Someone who carries out an enterprise, often at personal financial risk
- [ ] d. Someone who works in the Patent Office

4 How is a public corporation financed?

- [ ] a. By general taxation, in the form of Treasury grants
- [ ] b. By bank loans
- [ ] c. By public donation
- [ ] d. By voluntary payments

5 What is retained profit?

- [ ] a. Profit that is held back and not distributed as dividends to shareholders
- [ ] b. Profit that is not declared to the Inland Revenue
- [ ] c. A reduction in the cost of raw materials
- [ ] d. Limiting the amount of stock sold

6 If a company wanted to make use of a long-term source of capital, which of the following would it do?

- [ ] a. Request an overdraft
- [ ] b. Use a credit card
- [ ] c. Invest in stocks and shares
- [ ] d. Take out a loan

7 What does leasing equipment allow a company to do?

- ☐ a. Purchase the equipment quickly
- ☐ b. Rent, rather than purchase, the equipment
- ☐ c. Pay in instalments
- ☐ d. Test the equipment before spending any capital

8 How is the cash-flow cycle defined?

- ☐ a. As staff salaries
- ☐ b. As the number of invoices that await payment
- ☐ c. As the amount of money a company has in the bank
- ☐ d. As the continuous movement of cash in and out of a business

9 What is the break-even point?

- ☐ a. Increase in a company's productivity
- ☐ b. Reduction of employee wages
- ☐ c. Level of output where total cost and total revenue are the same
- ☐ d. When production levels remain stable

10 What does credit control mean?

- ☐ a. A company chooses to use its overdraft facilities
- ☐ b. A fixed number of organizations are allowed to borrow money
- ☐ c. A company limits the number of organizations obtaining credit
- ☐ d. An organization monitors the collection of money owed to it

11 What does a business plan do for a company?

- ☐ a. Outlines its potential profit margins
- ☐ b. Plans its staffing requirements
- ☐ c. Produces a five-year investment plan
- ☐ d. Outlines the way it will attempt to achieve its objectives

12 What does a profit-and-loss account show?

- ☐ a. The total number of employees
- ☐ b. The number of financial transactions in a trading year
- ☐ c. The total amount of debt for the company
- ☐ d. The net profit after tax

13 What does the current ratio show?

- ☐ a. The relationship between assets and liabilities
- ☐ b. The ratio of employees to shareholders
- ☐ c. The amount of stock held at any given time
- ☐ d. The level of production each month

14 What does the dividend yield describe?

- ☐ a. The amount received by each shareholder as a percentage of the share price
- ☐ b. The amount each shareholder invests in the company
- ☐ c. The total value of assets
- ☐ d. The total amount of sales as a percentage of production

15 What does receivership involve?

☐ a. Each employee receives a pay bonus
☐ b. A company receives money for its products
☐ c. The board of directors decides to stop production
☐ d. A company's assets are sold by an independent body

External environment and business

16 Which organization operates within the primary sector?

☐ a. A mining company
☐ b. A school
☐ c. A museum
☐ d. A supermarket

17 Which of the following is an example of a business activity within the secondary sector?

☐ a. A fashion store
☐ b. A landscape gardener
☐ c. A car manufacturer
☐ d. A newsagent

18 Which activity do you associate with the tertiary sector?

☐ a. An insurance company
☐ b. A carpenter
☐ c. A dairy farm
☐ d. A thatcher

19 Which is an example of a consumer service?

☐ a. A newspaper
☐ b. A loaf of sliced bread
☐ c. A restaurant meal
☐ d. A computer

20 Which of the following is considered a service?

☐ a. A newspaper
☐ b. Public transport
☐ c. A bar of chocolate
☐ d. A television set

21 Which statement best describes the tertiary sector?

☐ a. It has experienced a rapid decline in employment
☐ b. It has provided an increase in job opportunities
☐ c. It has employed mainly temporary staff
☐ d. It has increased the production of cars

22 What effect does an increase in interest rates have?

☐ a. It increases production
☐ b. It increases the number of job opportunities
☐ c. It increases costs
☐ d. It increases a company's profit margin

23 What is e-commerce?

☐ a. Related to an increase in food additives
☐ b. Trading using the Internet
☐ c. Employment opportunities
☐ d. Extra profits

24 Near to what would an industry specializing in the assembly of technical equipment locate?

☐ a. A power station
☐ b. An industrial estate
☐ c. A railway station
☐ d. A supply of skilled labour

25 What does an increase in the tax on fuel cause?

- [ ] a. Additional costs to companies
- [ ] b. New government legislation
- [ ] c. Reduced consumption
- [ ] d. Increased profits for petrol companies

26 Which is the most likely factor in deciding on the location of a new cinema complex?

- [ ] a. Proximity to customers
- [ ] b. Availability of natural resources
- [ ] c. Availability of a workforce
- [ ] d. Proximity to other businesses

27 A business's costs increase as a result of government intervention in tackling pollution. What is the business being affected by?

- [ ] a. Declining demand
- [ ] b. Competition
- [ ] c. Reduced sales
- [ ] d. Legal constraints

28 What would be an ideal location for a distribution company?

- [ ] a. Close to a large shopping centre
- [ ] b. Close to a housing estate
- [ ] c. In a rural area
- [ ] d. Close to an integrated transport network

29 A company places a misleading advert in a magazine. Which organization is responsible for dealing with consumer complaints?

- [ ] a. Trading Standards Office
- [ ] b. Citizens' Advice Bureau
- [ ] c. Trade Union Congress
- [ ] d. Advertising Standards Authority

30 Which piece of legislation attempts to prevent retailers providing incorrect information concerning goods?

- [ ] a. Factories Act
- [ ] b. Trade Descriptions Act
- [ ] c. Sex Discrimination Act
- [ ] d. Health and Safety Act

31 Why would people be willing to spend more of their disposable income on goods?

- [ ] a. The product is scarce
- [ ] b. The advertising campaign was successful
- [ ] c. Unemployment is increasing
- [ ] d. Interest rates have been reduced

32 How can consumer demand for goods and services be increased?

- [ ] a. By increasing interest rates
- [ ] b. By increasing advertising
- [ ] c. By increasing prices
- [ ] d. By increasing profit

Ownership and business operations

33 What does a teleworker do?

- [ ] a. Assembles electronic equipment
- [ ] b. Works from home and communicates with the main office via a data link
- [ ] c. Conducts market research
- [ ] d. Repairs televisions

34 What is the main purpose of a sole trader?

- [ ] a. To make a profit
- [ ] b. To increase consumer choice
- [ ] c. To decrease unemployment
- [ ] d. To limit employment opportunities

35 What is the main objective of a public-sector business?

- [ ] a. To reduce competition
- [ ] b. To provide a service to the public
- [ ] c. To provide information to the public
- [ ] d. To monitor population trends

36 What is the main purpose of a charity?

- [ ] a. To make a profit
- [ ] b. To aid a particular cause
- [ ] c. To increase consumer choice
- [ ] d. To sell secondhand goods

37 Which of the following are the owners of a public limited company?

- [ ] a. The government
- [ ] b. The local education authority
- [ ] c. The partners
- [ ] d. The shareholders

38 A group of solicitors usually operates as what?

- [ ] a. A franchise
- [ ] b. A private limited company
- [ ] c. A public limited company
- [ ] d. A partnership

39 In which type of business do the owners have unlimited liability?

- [ ] a. Public limited company
- [ ] b. Sole trader
- [ ] c. Local authority
- [ ] d. Private limited company

40 What do the majority of private limited companies have in common?

- [ ] a. The company cannot employ temporary workers
- [ ] b. They do not have to produce annual accounts
- [ ] c. The shareholders have limited liability
- [ ] d. They have less than one hundred employees

41 Who are the **main** decision-makers within a public limited company?

- [ ] a. The chief executive
- [ ] b. The board of directors
- [ ] c. The Inland Revenue
- [ ] d. The government

42 Which of the following is the most appropriate description for a business where one person decides on policy?

- [ ] a. Partnership
- [ ] b. Local authority
- [ ] c. Sole trader
- [ ] d. Private limited company

43 A business's market share decreases after a rival company begins to market similar products. What is this is known as?

- [ ] a. Limited liability
- [ ] b. Competition
- [ ] c. Increased cost
- [ ] d. Falling customer demand

44 Which activity is the most likely to reduce the number of customer complaints?

- [ ] a. Increased sponsorship
- [ ] b. Advertising
- [ ] c. After-sales service
- [ ] d. Free samples

45 What is a company with factories or offices in several countries known as?

- [ ] a. A multinational
- [ ] b. A local business
- [ ] c. A European concern
- [ ] d. A national company

46 What has a company done when it is considered to have experienced growth?

- [ ] a. Reduced costs
- [ ] b. Increased the price of its products
- [ ] c. Increased its market share
- [ ] d. Increased its range of products

47 What are the organizations The Samaritans, Oxfam, and Shelter examples of?

- [ ] a. Organizations that make a profit
- [ ] b. Organizations that provide a charitable service
- [ ] c. Organizations that are controlled by the government
- [ ] d. Organizations that provide information for local authorities

48 Which of the following is a nonprofit-making organization?

- [ ] a. A charity
- [ ] b. A franchise
- [ ] c. A wholesaler
- [ ] d. A multinational

49 How would a computer company aim to gain the largest share of the market?

- [ ] a. By producing the most computers
- [ ] b. By selling the most computers
- [ ] c. By advertising
- [ ] d. By producing the widest range of computers

50 What influence is a consumer group most likely to have on a business organization?

- [ ] a. Decrease sales
- [ ] b. Affect the way the organization operates
- [ ] c. Increase wages
- [ ] d. Increase competition

51 What will a company carry out to estimate the potential demand for a product?

- [ ] a. A programme of training for its employees
- [ ] b. A financial audit
- [ ] c. An advertising campaign
- [ ] d. Market research

52 To meet the seasonal demand for its products, who will an ice-cream manufacturer employ?

- [ ] a. An advertising agency
- [ ] b. Unskilled staff
- [ ] c. Temporary staff
- [ ] d. Permanent staff

53 What will a company do to maintain its profitability?

- [ ] a. Reduce its sales
- [ ] b. Reduce its advertising
- [ ] c. Reduce its production
- [ ] d. Reduce its costs

54 What is one of the main objectives of a company?

- ☐ a. To reduce the cost of raw materials
- ☐ b. To employ a limited number of employees
- ☐ c. To make a profit
- ☐ d. To increase consumer awareness of its products

55 If the manufacturer of car components has had to install specialized safety equipment as a result of new legislation, what is this called?

- ☐ a. Social objective
- ☐ b. Legal objective
- ☐ c. Financial objective
- ☐ d. Environmental objective

Management of people

56 What is the **main** role of a manager?

- ☐ a. To make sure that every employee is working at all times
- ☐ b. To carry out the policies of the board of directors
- ☐ c. To make financial decisions
- ☐ d. To increase profitability

57 What is the **main** advantage of employing part-time staff?

- ☐ a. They are cheap to employ
- ☐ b. They provide flexibility for management
- ☐ c. They do not belong to a trade union
- ☐ d. They do not demand regular pay rises

58 Which of the following is the most appropriate description of an organization where there are as few levels of authority as possible?

- ☐ a. Centralized
- ☐ b. Hierarchical
- ☐ c. Functional
- ☐ d. Flat

59 Which department is responsible for keeping confidential staff records?

- ☐ a. Personnel
- ☐ b. Administration
- ☐ c. Accounts
- ☐ d. Marketing

60 Which department is responsible for providing clerical support to other departments?

- ☐ a. Customer services
- ☐ b. Administration
- ☐ c. Maintenance
- ☐ d. Accounts

61 Why are organizations divided into departments?

- ☐ a. Specialized departments enable the organization to be more effective
- ☐ b. Staff can work in other departments
- ☐ c. The board of directors can delegate responsibility
- ☐ d. It reduces the problem of staff absences

62 What is the major benefit of improved management and employee relationships?

- ☐ a. A reduction in staff costs
- ☐ b. An increase in staff motivation

☐ c. An increase in employment opportunities

☐ d. A reduction in training

63 What is improved by the introduction of team-working into an organization?

☐ a. Health and safety

☐ b. Marketing

☐ c. Productivity

☐ d. Customer services

64 What does an organization seek to improve when it introduces an employee incentive scheme?

☐ a. Training

☐ b. Motivation

☐ c. Customer relations

☐ d. Absenteeism

65 What type of working arrangement allows an employee to alter the time that they start and finish each day's work?

☐ a. Part-time

☐ b. Flexitime

☐ c. Permanent

☐ d. Fixed-term

66 Why does an organization introduce a staff induction programme?

☐ a. To increase profits

☐ b. To increase efficiency

☐ c. To increase overtime

☐ d. To increase competition

67 To which of the following would a case of unfair dismissal be brought?

☐ a. Health and Safety Committee

☐ b. Trade union

☐ c. European Court of Justice

☐ d. Advisory, Conciliation, and Arbitration Service

68 What has an employer the right to expect each employee to work?

☐ a. Without safety equipment

☐ b. Overtime

☐ c. Weekends

☐ d. To their contract

69 In which document would an employee's holiday entitlement be written?

☐ a. Equal opportunities policy

☐ b. Health and safety document

☐ c. Contract of employment

☐ d. Job description

70 If a male employee is paid more than a female employee for doing the same work, what is this called?

☐ a. Age discrimination

☐ b. Sex discrimination

☐ c. Religious discrimination

☐ d. Race discrimination

71 Which of the following does an employer have a legal right to deduct from an employee's wages?

☐ a. Trade union fees

☐ b. Holiday pay

☐ c. Sick pay

☐ d. Income tax

72 Which of the following should be contained within a written contract of employment?

☐ a. Trade union details

☐ b. Details of overtime arrangements

☐ c. Health and safety details
☐ d. Expected working hours

73 What is a personnel department responsible for?

☐ a. Market research
☐ b. Filing invoices
☐ c. Maintenance
☐ d. Staff training

Production and costing

74 A firm's direct costs are those that can be what?

☐ a. Directly linked to particular product lines
☐ b. Written off as a loss
☐ c. Calculated monthly
☐ d. Estimated

75 Which of these statements is true about a firm's indirect costs?

☐ a. They do not relate to one particular product
☐ b. They can be used to estimate productivity
☐ c. They relate only to time lost through machine breakdown
☐ d. They are calculated annually

76 What would be a definition of an opportunity cost?

☐ a. The total cost of promoting a range of products
☐ b. Where a firm recognizes an opportunity to make a quick profit
☐ c. The result of purchasing raw materials cheaply

☐ d. Where a firm has to ignore one opportunity to take advantage of another

77 Which of the following would normally be produced using mass production techniques?

☐ a. Handmade furniture
☐ b. Houses
☐ c. A watercolour painting
☐ d. Televisions

78 Why would a firm decide to use batch production?

☐ a. To provide a sample product
☐ b. To utilize skilled labour
☐ c. To keep costs under control
☐ d. To develop an existing product

79 What is 'just-in-time' manufacturing used for?

☐ a. To reduce the cost of products
☐ b. To maintain minimum stock levels and reorder in response to production levels
☐ c. To reduce the number of employees working on a product
☐ d. To maintain a high level of stock

80 Which of the following define the factors of production?

☐ a. Capital, choice, cost, and credit
☐ b. Price, promotion, place, and product
☐ c. Capital, enterprise, land, and labour
☐ d. Scarcity, choice, resources, and labour

Marketing and distribution

81 What would market segmentation be used to do?

- ☐ a. Classify producers by type
- ☐ b. Classify consumers by type
- ☐ c. Produce product statistics
- ☐ d. Produce consumer statistics

82 If a company used a SWOT analysis, what would it be defining?

- ☐ a. Supply, wages, overheads, and taxation
- ☐ b. Supervisors, workers, officers, and trainees
- ☐ c. Strengths, weaknesses, offices, and taxation
- ☐ d. Strengths, weaknesses, opportunities, and threats

83 What consumer characteristic is **most likely** to influence the demand for high-performance cars?

- ☐ a. Employment
- ☐ b. Age
- ☐ c. Lifestyle
- ☐ d. Gender

84 A company would use a consumer panel to do what?

- ☐ a. Receive a sample product and give a detailed report
- ☐ b. Suggest a price for the product
- ☐ c. Offer free samples to other potential consumers
- ☐ d. Comment on the design of the product

85 What are the three stages of a product's life cycle?

- ☐ a. Growth, consumption, and development
- ☐ b. Research, production, price, and sales
- ☐ c. Growth, maturity, and decline
- ☐ d. Production, consumption, and regeneration

86 What are the 'four Ps' that make up the marketing mix?

- ☐ a. Price, position, profit, and placement
- ☐ b. Product, price, place, and promotion
- ☐ c. Price, population, proximity, and profit
- ☐ d. Product, place, position, and platform

87 Which of the following pricing policies would be considered 'high price'?

- ☐ a. Skimming
- ☐ b. Promoting
- ☐ c. Maximizing
- ☐ d. Positioning

88 Why would a consumer be willing to pay a high price for a certain product?

- ☐ a. It is a status symbol
- ☐ b. Everybody else has one
- ☐ c. They can afford it
- ☐ d. It is available on credit

89 Why would a company use persuasive promotion?

☐ a. To convince people that they need the product
☐ b. To increase market share
☐ c. To increase production
☐ d. Because no one will buy their products

90 What are the main channels of distribution?

☐ a. Researchers, developers, manufacturers, and buyers
☐ b. Researchers, manufacturers, wholesalers, and retailers
☐ c. Developers, manufacturers, buyers, and retailers
☐ d. Manufacturers, wholesalers, retailers, and consumers

Religious Education

Questions

Buddhism

1 How did enlightenment come to the Buddha?

- [ ] a. By reading sacred writings
- [ ] b. By asking ascetics important questions
- [ ] c. Through deep meditation
- [ ] d. Through prayer and chanting

2 What phrase is used to explain the terms dukkha, samudaya, nirodha, and magga?

- [ ] a. The Four Noble Truths
- [ ] b. The Four Precepts
- [ ] c. The Four Marks of Existence
- [ ] d. The Four Paths to Enlightenment

3 Which is the earliest form of Buddhism?

- [ ] a. Tibetan
- [ ] b. Theravada
- [ ] c. Mahayana
- [ ] d. Pure Land

4 What is the name given to the three collections of Buddhist scriptures?

- [ ] a. Sutta Pitaka
- [ ] b. Tripitaka
- [ ] c. Rig Veda
- [ ] d. Vinaya Pitaka

5 Which festival celebrates the birth, enlightenment, and passing away of the Buddha?

- [ ] a. Uposatha days
- [ ] b. Wesak
- [ ] c. Asala
- [ ] d. Divali

6 Where was Gautama Siddhartha said to have been born?

- [ ] a. Lumbini
- [ ] b. Anaradhapura
- [ ] c. Varanasi
- [ ] d. Bodh Gaya

7 When Gautama Siddhartha was born, what is he believed to have done?

- [ ] a. Walked seven steps in each of the four directions
- [ ] b. Said a prayer to the gods Indra and Brahma

☐ c. Picked lotus flowers for the gods Indra and Brahma

☐ d. Looked at his mother and announced his name

8 What did Gautama Siddhartha's father want him to become when he grew up?

☐ a. A holy man
☐ b. A champion warrior
☐ c. A great healer
☐ d. A great emperor

9 What did Gautama Siddhartha see that made him want to leave the palace to begin his search for enlightenment?

☐ a. Three old women, begging
☐ b. A group of travelling players
☐ c. Four Signs
☐ d. Four Noble Truths

10 Where did Gautama Siddhartha achieve enlightenment?

☐ a. At the deer park at Varanasi
☐ b. Under the bodhi tree at Buddh Gaya
☐ c. At Lumbini
☐ d. In the palace grounds

11 What does the term 'Buddha' mean?

☐ a. The Noble One
☐ b. The Enlightened One
☐ c. The Chosen One
☐ d. The Holy One

12 The Dalai Lama is the spiritual leader of which group of Buddhists?

☐ a. Pure Land Buddhists
☐ b. Thai Buddhists

☐ c. Tibetan Buddhists
☐ d. Zen Buddhists

Christianity

13 What phrase is used to describe God the Father, the Son, and the Holy Spirit?

☐ a. The Holy Tribune
☐ b. The Holy Triune
☐ c. The Holy Trinity
☐ d. The Holy Triangle

14 According to Jesus, what is the 'Golden Rule' for all Christians?

☐ a. All people are important because they are Children of God
☐ b. Love God with all your heart, soul, and strength and love your neighbour as yourself
☐ c. You must be perfect, just as your Father in heaven is perfect
☐ d. Do not judge others, so that God will not judge you

15 What do Christians mean when they say that 'life is sacred'?

☐ a. It happened because of evolution
☐ b. It is a gift from God
☐ c. It is a result of sex between a man and a woman
☐ d. It means that people are responsible for each other

16 What is the word 'agape' used by Christians to describe?

☐ a. Christian love
☐ b. Love of friends

☐ c. Sexual love
☐ d. Family love

17 Which method of contraception would be permitted by Roman Catholics?

☐ a. The IUD (coil)
☐ b. The pill
☐ c. The withdrawal method
☐ d. The condom

18 Which statement best expresses the Roman Catholic attitude to divorce?

☐ a. It is right if the two people are always arguing
☐ b. It is wrong because Jesus said, 'What God has joined together, man must not separate'
☐ c. It is wrong because children want their parents to stay together
☐ d. It is right if the two people fall out of love with each other

19 What is the operation which results in 'the premature expulsion of the foetus from the womb'?

☐ a. Abortion
☐ b. Conception
☐ c. Contraception
☐ d. Euthanasia

20 Why is euthanasia a difficult issue for Christians?

☐ a. Because the person suffering may not be able to say what s/he wants
☐ b. Because they believe that life is sacred and only God can take it away

☐ c. Because they believe it is a waste of money to keep terminally-ill people alive
☐ d. Because they believe it would be better to die than be handicapped

21 Which statement best expresses the Christian view of money?

☐ a. You cannot serve God and money
☐ b. Money cannot buy love
☐ c. Money gives pleasure all the time
☐ d. Remember that time is money

22 Who do Christians regard as 'the Son of God'?

☐ a. Jesus
☐ b. Moses
☐ c. Joshua
☐ d. John the Baptist

23 Which answer best describes the importance of the Old Testament to Christians?

☐ a. It contains the Ten Commandments
☐ b. It describes the escape of the Jews from Egypt
☐ c. It foretells the coming of Jesus, the Messiah
☐ d. It tells the story of the creation of the Universe

24 What can be found in the New Testament?

☐ a. The prophecies concerning the Suffering Servant of God
☐ b. The account of the life of Jesus and the birth of the Church

☐ c. The account of King David's entry into Jerusalem
☐ d. The Pentateuch

25 What does 'gospel' mean?

☐ a. Good times
☐ b. Teaching
☐ c. Christian letters
☐ d. Good news

26 Which Gospel is thought to have been the first one written?

☐ a. Mark
☐ b. Luke
☐ c. Matthew
☐ d. John

27 What does Jesus say about divorce in Mark's Gospel?

☐ a. A man may divorce his wife by giving her a divorce notice
☐ b. A man who divorces his wife, except for the reason of unfaithfulness, and marries another, commits adultery
☐ c. A man may divorce his wife for whatever reason he wishes
☐ d. A man who divorces his wife and marries another woman commits adultery

28 In Luke's Gospel, who were first to be told of the birth of Jesus?

☐ a. King Herod
☐ b. Wise men
☐ c. Shepherds
☐ d. Farmers

29 In the parable of 'The Good Samaritan', who was injured?

☐ a. A Roman

☐ b. A Jew
☐ c. A Christian
☐ d. A Samaritan

30 What is the relationship between the Samaritan and the others in the story?

☐ a. They are friends
☐ b. They are enemies
☐ c. They are countrymen
☐ d. They are strangers

31 Which disciple denied ever knowing Jesus?

☐ a. Judas
☐ b. James
☐ c. Peter
☐ d. Thomas

32 Which disciple betrayed Jesus in the Garden of Gethsemane?

☐ a. John
☐ b. Judas
☐ c. Peter
☐ d. Andrew

33 What did Joseph of Arimathea ask Pilate to do?

☐ a. To let him carry Jesus' cross on the way to the crucifixion
☐ b. To give him Jesus' robe
☐ c. To let him keep watch at Jesus' tomb
☐ d. To give him Jesus' body for burial in a tomb

34 Who found Jesus' empty tomb?

☐ a. Disciples
☐ b. Roman soldiers
☐ c. Women who had followed Jesus
☐ d. Pharisees

35 Which Christian festival celebrates the visit of the Wise Men to the baby Jesus?

- ☐ a. Pentecost
- ☐ b. Advent
- ☐ c. Epiphany
- ☐ d. Christmas

36 Which event in the life of Jesus is remembered on Good Friday?

- ☐ a. His resurrection from the dead
- ☐ b. His Last Supper with the disciples
- ☐ c. His crucifixion and death
- ☐ d. His entry into Jerusalem

37 Which US Christian minister was dedicated to trying to change the way that African-Americans were treated?

- ☐ a. Maximillian Kolbe
- ☐ b. Oscar Romero
- ☐ c. Martin Luther King
- ☐ d. Nelson Mandela

38 Which Commandment might a Christian pacifist think would be broken by going to war?

- ☐ a. Keep the Sabbath holy
- ☐ b. You shall not blaspheme
- ☐ c. You shall not kill
- ☐ d. Do not lie

39 Who was awarded the Nobel Prize for Peace for work with the sick and dying in Calcutta?

- ☐ a. Martin Luther King
- ☐ b. Mother Teresa
- ☐ c. Father Camilo Torres
- ☐ d. Archbishop Tutu

40 What do Christians call the promises they make at a marriage service?

- ☐ a. Marriage statements
- ☐ b. Marriage oaths
- ☐ c. Marriage vows
- ☐ d. Marriage declarations

41 Why is baptism important to Christians?

- ☐ a. It shows that men and women are equal
- ☐ b. It is a demonstration of their belief in Jesus and is the rite of initiation into the Church
- ☐ c. It is a chance to have a christening party to celebrate being a Christian
- ☐ d. It means that they will go straight to Heaven when they die

42 Why is a funeral service important to Christians?

- ☐ a. It expresses the hope of resurrection to eternal life
- ☐ b. It celebrates the life a person has led
- ☐ c. It allows a show of grief without feeling embarrassed
- ☐ d. It allows family and friends a chance to say goodbye

Hinduism

43 Where did Hinduism originate?

- ☐ a. Pakistan
- ☐ b. India
- ☐ c. Sri Lanka
- ☐ d. China

44 Who was the spiritual and political leader of India in its struggle for independence from the Britain?

- ☐ a. Mahatma Gandhi
- ☐ b. Nehru
- ☐ c. Banda Singh
- ☐ d. Indira Gandhi

45 What does 'Brahman' mean?

- ☐ a. The ultimate reality or world soul
- ☐ b. The one and only god
- ☐ c. The true being
- ☐ d. The creative power

46 Which Hindu deity has a 'third eye' in the centre of his forehead?

- ☐ a. Brahma
- ☐ b. Shiva
- ☐ c. Vishnu
- ☐ d. Ganesha

47 What term is used to describe how the actions in a previous life determine the new body into which a soul is reborn?

- ☐ a. Coincidence
- ☐ b. Yoga
- ☐ c. Karma
- ☐ d. Nirvana

48 What is the word used to describe the deity Vishnu's taking on human form, such as in the figure of Rama?

- ☐ a. Avatar
- ☐ b. Moksha
- ☐ c. Atman
- ☐ d. Maya

49 How is the Hindu deity Ganesh portrayed?

- ☐ a. As the deity who removes obstacles and has an elephant's head
- ☐ b. As the deity who is known as the monkey god
- ☐ c. As the deity who carries a trident with a snake coiled around his neck
- ☐ d. As the deity who wears a garland of human skulls and brings war and disease

50 What is the name of the first of the Hindu scriptures, which contain spiritual and scientific knowledge?

- ☐ a. Bhagavad Gita
- ☐ b. Yajur Veda
- ☐ c. Mahabharata
- ☐ d. Rig Veda

51 What is one of the reasons for the festival of Divali?

- ☐ a. It is concerned with the worship of the goddess Durga
- ☐ b. It commemorates the battle between gods and demons over the nectar of immortality
- ☐ c. It marks the return of Rama to his rightful kingdom after the defeat of Ravana
- ☐ d. It is associated with Krishna who killed the demoness Putana

52 Why is 'puja' (worship) performed in the home at Divali?

- ☐ a. So as not to upset the Hindu deities
- ☐ b. To show respect for the Hindu deities
- ☐ c. To ask Ganesh to remove obstacles
- ☐ d. To encourage Lakshmi, goddess of wealth, to bring good fortune during the coming year

53 Which ceremony is performed by some Hindus when a boy is between 8 and 12 years old?

- ☐ a. Confirmation
- ☐ b. Sacred Thread ceremony
- ☐ c. Bar mitzvah
- ☐ d. Circumcision

54 What can happen once a Hindu has died and the body has been reduced to ashes?

- ☐ a. It marks the end of existence
- ☐ b. The soul can choose another body to inhabit
- ☐ c. The soul is able to live in another body
- ☐ d. The soul is released to be with God in heaven

Islam

55 How was Islam founded?

- ☐ a. Abraham founded Islam when he made an agreement with Allah
- ☐ b. Islam was founded by Moses
- ☐ c. Muslims believe there is no founder, but that Islam has always existed and always will

- ☐ d. Islam was founded by the angel Gabriel who spoke to Muhammad

56 Who was Khadija?

- ☐ a. The first wife of the Prophet
- ☐ b. An important follower of the Prophet
- ☐ c. The mother of the Prophet
- ☐ d. The youngest sister of the Prophet

57 What was the Hijrah?

- ☐ a. The emigration of the Prophet and his followers from Mecca to Medina
- ☐ b. A pilgrimage to Mecca
- ☐ c. The Prophet's triumphal entry into Mecca in 8 AH
- ☐ d. A journey to the Ka'bah

58 Why do Muslims describe Muhammad as 'The Seal of the Prophets'?

- ☐ a. Because no more messengers of Allah have come or ever will
- ☐ b. Because he is the only prophet
- ☐ c. Because he taught submission to Allah
- ☐ d. Because he signed an agreement to spread the Word of Allah

59 How are Muslims called to prayer?

- ☐ a. By bugles blown outside the mosque
- ☐ b. By a person called the Mu'adhin (muezzin)
- ☐ c. By messages on the local radio stations
- ☐ d. By a peal of bells from the tower of the mosque

60 What is meant by the Five Pillars of Islam?

☐ a. They refer to the different prayer positions
☐ b. They contain sacred writings and stories of the prophets
☐ c. They are a description of the way to wash before prayer
☐ d. They refer to the actions a Muslim must perform if there is to be a strong foundation to faith

61 What is 'salah'?

☐ a. A declaration of faith
☐ b. Fasting
☐ c. Pilgrimage
☐ d. Prayer

62 What is the name given to the divine book revealed to the Prophet Muhammad?

☐ a. The Sunna
☐ b. The Sirah
☐ c. The Koran
☐ d. The Hadith

63 When should Muslims fast during the month of Ramadan?

☐ a. They do not fast at all
☐ b. For at least a week
☐ c. Every day from just before dawn until sunset
☐ d. For two hours each afternoon

64 Which festival follows the month of Ramadan?

☐ a. Eid ul-Fitr
☐ b. Ibadah
☐ c. Eid Mubarak
☐ d. Eid ul-Adha

65 What event does a Muslim hope will happen at least once in a lifetime?

☐ a. Salah
☐ b. Zakah
☐ c. Hajj
☐ d. Saum

66 What is the Kaaba?

☐ a. A pilgrimage to Mecca
☐ b. A modern mosque in Saudi Arabia
☐ c. A cube-shaped structure in the centre of the grand mosque in Mecca
☐ d. The spot where pilgrims collect pebbles to throw at the pillars at Mina

Judaism

67 In Genesis, who made the covenant with God?

☐ a. Jacob
☐ b. Isaac
☐ c. Abraham
☐ d. Moses

68 Who received the Ten Commandments on Mount Sinai?

☐ a. Abraham
☐ b. Joseph
☐ c. Moses
☐ d. Benjamin

69 Who was the first king of Israel?

☐ a. Josiah
☐ b. Solomon
☐ c. Saul
☐ d. David

70 What can be found at Yad Vashem?

- [ ] a. A monument dedicated to Moses
- [ ] b. The remains of the Temple
- [ ] c. The remains of Solomon's garden
- [ ] d. A memorial to the six million Jews who died in the Holocaust

71 Which major Jewish prayer begins, 'Hear, O Israel, the Lord our God, the Lord is One'?

- [ ] a. The Shema
- [ ] b. The Aleinu
- [ ] c. The Siddur
- [ ] d. The Kiddush

72 What are tefillin?

- [ ] a. Small leather boxes containing passages from the Torah
- [ ] b. The fringes on the corners of the prayer shawl
- [ ] c. Prayer shawls with fringes
- [ ] d. Four-sided spinning tops used for a game at Hanukkah

73 In Judaism, what is the name of the day of spiritual renewal and rest that begins at sunset on Friday?

- [ ] a. Sabbath
- [ ] b. Purim
- [ ] c. Pesach
- [ ] d. Shavuot

74 What is the name of the small box found on the doorpost of a Jewish home and containing the Shema?

- [ ] a. Yad
- [ ] b. Kippah
- [ ] c. Menorah
- [ ] d. Mezuzah

75 What is the name given to the collection of 24 books of the Jewish scriptures?

- [ ] a. The Ketuvim
- [ ] b. The Torah
- [ ] c. The Talmud
- [ ] d. The Tenakh

76 What is Yom Kippur?

- [ ] a. The festival commemorating the exodus from Egypt
- [ ] b. The day to commemorate the Shoah
- [ ] c. The festival celebrating the rescue of Persian Jews as told in the book of Esther
- [ ] d. The Day of Atonement, when Jews fast, confess their sins to God, and ask forgiveness

77 When does a Jewish father usually say, 'Blessed is he who has released me from responsibility for this child'?

- [ ] a. At his son's bar mitzvah
- [ ] b. At his son's wedding
- [ ] c. When his son leaves home
- [ ] d. When his son starts school

78 What is shiva?

- [ ] a. Care for the world and environment
- [ ] b. The seven holy names of God
- [ ] c. A hand-held pointer used in reading the Sefer Torah
- [ ] d. Seven days of mourning following the death of a relative

Sikhism

79 How was Guru Nanak brought up?

☐ a. As one who respected all faiths
☐ b. As a Kshatriya and orthodox Hind
☐ c. As a boy destined to become a great holy man
☐ d. As a Muslim

80 Who founded Sikhism?

☐ a. Guru Har Gobind
☐ b. Guru Nanak
☐ c. Guru Gobind Singh
☐ d. Guru Arjan

81 What did Guru Gobind Singh ask the thousands of Sikhs gathered at Anandpur in 1699?

☐ a. He asked them to pray for guidance
☐ b. He asked who would give his head for the guru
☐ c. He asked them to give money to support the faith
☐ d. He asked who would join his army of Sikhs

82 Which of the 'five Ks' is the kara?

☐ a. The uncut hair that is a visible sign of allegiance
☐ b. The steel bracelet that is worn as a charm against evil
☐ c. The sword symbolizing the Sikh's determination to fight for right
☐ d. The comb symbolizing the order, discipline, and control of a true Sikh

83 Which basic statement of belief begins, 'There is One God, Eternal Truth is His Name'?

☐ a. The Ardas
☐ b. The Gurbani
☐ c. The Nam Simran
☐ d. The Mul Mantra

84 Who was the first guru to be born a Sikh and also the first Sikh martyr?

☐ a. Guru Tej Bahadur
☐ b. Guru Har Krishen
☐ c. Guru Arjan
☐ d. Guru Nanak

85 Which temple, situated in the middle of a lake, do many Sikhs visit?

☐ a. The Golden Temple at Anandpur
☐ b. The temple at Nankana Sahib, the birthplace of Guru Nanak
☐ c. The Akal Takht Temple
☐ d. The Golden Temple at Amritsar

86 What is the name of the collection of Sikh scriptures that was given its final form by Guru Gobind Singh?

☐ a. The Granthi
☐ b. The Dasam Granth
☐ c. The Janamsakhi
☐ d. The Guru Granth Sahib

87 What is the name of the festival that celebrates the formation of the Khalsa?

☐ a. Hola Mohalla
☐ b. Guru Nanak's birthday
☐ c. Baisakhi
☐ d. Divali

88 Which story is told in Sikh communities at Divali?

☐ a. The story of the martyrdom of Guru Tej Bahadur, the ninth guru

☐ b. The story of the martyrdom of Guru Arjan, the fifth guru

☐ c. The story of Har Gobind, the sixth guru

☐ d. The story of the birth of guru Nanak

89 What is the langar?

☐ a. Sanctified food distributed at Sikh ceremonies

☐ b. The gurdwara dining hall and the communal meal served in it

☐ c. Sanctified liquid made of sugar and water, used in initiation ceremonies

☐ d. A small platform on which the scripture is placed

90 What is 'akhand path', which may be commissioned by families shortly after the birth of a child?

☐ a. Prayers said in the gurdwara to celebrate the birth

☐ b. The continuous reading of the Guru Granth Sahib from beginning to end

☐ c. A naming ceremony in the gurdwara attended by all the relatives

☐ d. Giving the infant a drop of sugared water from the tip of a kirpan

Answers

ENGLISH

1 d	2 c	3 c	4 b
5 d	6 d	7 b	8 b
9 d	10 c	11 a	12 d
13 a	14 b	15 b	16 b
17 c	18 d	19 a	20 d
21 c	22 d	23 d	24 b
25 c	26 a	27 a	28 d
29 c	30 d	31 a	32 a
33 c	34 c	35 c	36 d
37 a	38 c	39 b	40 c
41 a	42 c	43 b	44 d
45 a	46 b	47 c	48 c
49 d	50 a	51 d	52 b
53 a	54 a	55 a	56 d
57 b	58 c	59 a	60 c
61 b	62 c	63 b	64 a
65 b	66 d	67 d	68 b
69 d	70 b	71 c	72 c
73 c	74 d	75 b	76 d
77 c	78 d	79 a	80 d
81 a	82 d	83 d	84 b
85 d	86 d	87 c	88 c
89 b	90 c	91 c	92 d
93 b	94 d	95 b	96 a
97 b	98 a	99 c	
100 a	101 c	102 c	
103 a	104 c	105 c	
106 c	107 c	108 d	
109 b	110 b	111 d	
112 c	113 d	114 c	
115 d	116 d	117 d	
118 b	119 c	120 c	
121 b	122 d	123 a	
124 a	125 b	126 b	
127 a	128 a	129 d	
130 a	131 a	132 d	
133 a	134 b	135 b	
136 b	137 a	138 b	
139 c	140 c	141 d	
142 c	143 b	144 b	
145 d	146 d	147 c	
148 c	149 c	150 a	

MATHEMATICS

1 c	2 d	3 c	4 c
5 d	6 b	7 d	8 a
9 a	10 c	11 c	12 c
13 a	14 b	15 d	16 d
17 b	18 a	19 c	20 a
21 b	22 b	23 d	24 a
25 c	26 c	27 c	28 c
29 a	30 c	31 a	32 a
33 a	34 c	35 a	36 b
37 c	38 a	39 b	40 c
41 a	42 a	43 b	44 a
45 a	46 c	47 c	48 c
49 c	50 a	51 a	52 d
53 a	54 a	55 d	56 d
57 a	58 a	59 d	60 a
61 a	62 b	63 b	64 b
65 d	66 d	67 d	68 d
69 c	70 a	71 c	72 d
73 a	74 d	75 a	76 b
77 d	78 a	79 c	80 b
81 b	82 a	83 d	84 c
85 c	86 d	87 c	88 a
89 a	90 b	91 d	92 b
93 b	94 a	95 a	96 d
97 a	98 d	99 d	
100 d	101 b	102 d	
103 d	104 b	105 c	
106 d	107 d	108 c	
109 a	110 b	111 a	
112 d	113 a	114 d	
115 b	116 a	117 d	
118 a	119 c	120 b	
121 b	122 d	123 a	
124 a	125 a	126 d	
127 b	128 a	129 c	
130 b	131 b	132 c	
133 c	134 b	135 d	
136 d	137 a	138 b	
139 a	140 d	141 d	
142 b	143 b	144 a	
145 c	146 c	147 c	
148 b	149 d	150 a	
151 d	152 c	153 a	

BIOLOGY

1 a	2 a	3 d	4 b
5 d	6 b	7 b	8 a
9 d	10 d	11 c	12 b
13 b	14 d	15 c	16 b
17 c	18 d	19 c	20 d
21 d	22 b	23 c	24 d
25 b	26 d	27 b	28 a
29 c	30 b	31 a	32 b
33 b	34 c	35 d	36 d
37 c	38 a	39 b	40 a
41 d	42 c	43 b	44 b
45 a	46 c	47 d	48 c
49 b	50 d	51 b	52 b
53 c	54 c	55 d	56 d
57 b	58 c	59 d	60 a
61 d	62 c	63 c	64 b
65 c	66 a	67 d	68 d
69 b	70 b	71 a	72 b
73 a	74 a	75 a	76 d
77 d	78 b	79 d	80 a
81 c	82 d	83 b	84 c
85 b	86 a	87 a	88 c

89 c   90 c   91 c   92 d
93 d   94 c   95 c   96 c
97 c   98 a   99 c
100 b   101 d   102 b
103 d   104 c   105 b
106 c   107 c   108 c
109 b   110 d   111 c
112 c   113 c   114 c
115 a   116 b   117 a
118 c   119 a   120 b
121 a   122 c   123 d
124 d   125 b   126 d
127 c   128 a   129 b
130 a   131 c   132 d
133 b   134 a   135 d
136 c   137 d   138 c
139 c   140 c   141 a
142 b   143 d   144 a
145 c   146 a   147 c
148 d   149 b   150 a

CHEMISTRY

1 a   2 c   3 c   4 c
5 a   6 a   7 c   8 c
9 b   10 c   11 b   12 a
13 a   14 d   15 c   16 c
17 a   18 c   19 c   20 a
21 a   22 b   23 d   24 b
25 a   26 d   27 c   28 a
29 a   30 c   31 a   32 b
33 b   34 c   35 b   36 b
37 a   38 c   39 d   40 b
41 a   42 d   43 a   44 d
45 a   46 b   47 c   48 c
49 b   50 c   51 d   52 d
53 c   54 a   55 d   56 d
57 d   58 d   59 c   60 a
61 b   62 a   63 a   64 a
65 d   66 d   67 b   68 b
69 c   70 c   71 b   72 a
73 a   74 c   75 b   76 c
77 d   78 a   79 a   80 a

81 b   82 b   83 d   84 b
85 b   86 a   87 b   88 b
89 a   90 c   91 c   92 a
93 b   94 b   95 d   96 d
97 d   98 b   99 a
100 c   101 b   102 b
103 b   104 d   105 a
106 c   107 c   108 b
109 c   110 c   111 c
112 c   113 a   114 c
115 b   116 a   117 d
118 b   119 b   120 d
121 b   122 c   123 a
124 b   125 d   126 d
127 b   128 d   129 a
130 b   131 d   132 a
133 c   134 a   135 a
136 c   137 a   138 d
139 b   140 d   141 c
142 d   143 b   144 d
145 d   146 b   147 a
148 a   149 a   150 c

PHYSICS

1 b   2 c   3 c   4 c
5 a   6 d   7 c   8 c
9 c   10 d   11 b   12 b
13 a   14 d   15 c   16 c
17 a   18 d   19 b   20 b
21 c   22 a   23 a   24 d
25 c   26 d   27 c   28 a
29 d   30 d   31 d   32 b
33 d   34 b   35 d   36 c
37 c   38 a   39 c   40 b
41 c   42 a   43 d   44 c
45 a   46 a   47 b   48 a
49 a   50 d   51 d   52 b
53 b   54 d   55 b   56 c
57 a   58 c   59 b   60 d
61 a   62 c   63 d   64 c
65 b   66 a   67 d   68 a
69 b   70 b   71 c   72 c

73 b   74 a   75 c   76 c
77 b   78 d   79 b   80 a
81 d   82 a   83 a   84 d
85 a   86 b   87 c   88 d
89 d   90 b   91 d   92 b
93 c   94 b   95 a   96 b
97 b   98 a   99 a
100 a   101 c   102 d
103 c   104 c   105 b
106 a   107 d   108 c
109 a   110 c   111 a
112 b   113 d   114 c
115 a   116 c   117 c
118 b   119 c   120 d
121 c   122 a   123 c
124 d   125 d   126 a
127 d   128 d   129 a
130 d   131 d   132 c
133 c   134 a   135 c
136 d   137 a   138 c
139 d   140 a   141 b
142 a   143 c   144 b
145 a   146 b   147 c
148 b   149 c   150 c

DESIGN AND TECHNOLOGY

1 a   2 c   3 a   4 d
5 d   6 a   7 a   8 c
9 a   10 a   11 a   12 b
13 a   14 b   15 d   16 a
17 c   18 a   19 d   20 d
21 b   22 a   23 c   24 d
25 d   26 d   27 a   28 b
29 c   30 b   31 b   32 a
33 d   34 d   35 d   36 c
37 b   38 c   39 d   40 a
41 a   42 a   43 d   44 c
45 a   46 c   47 b   48 b
49 b   50 b   51 d   52 d
53 d   54 c   55 b   56 d
57 c   58 a   59 b   60 b

61 c 62 c 63 c 64 b
65 d 66 b 67 b 68 c
69 d 70 d 71 d 72 b
73 c 74 d 75 a 76 c
77 c 78 b 79 c 80 c
81 d 82 b 83 b 84 c
85 c 86 a 87 a 88 a
89 d 90 c

INFORMATION AND COM-MUNICATION TECHNOLOGY (ICT)

1 a   2 a   3 c   4 b
5 b   6 c   7 c   8 c
9 a   10 a 11 a 12 a
13 a 14 c 15 b 16 c
17 d 18 a 19 a 20 c
21 a 22 a 23 d 24 b
25 a 26 b 27 c 28 d
29 a 30 c 31 d 32 b
33 a 34 a 35 d 36 d
37 c 38 d 39 c 40 b
41 c 42 d 43 d 44 c
45 a 46 a 47 d 48 a
49 c 50 c 51 d 52 b
53 c 54 c 55 b 56 b
57 b 58 b 59 d 60 b
61 a 62 b 63 c 64 c
65 b 66 c 67 c 68 d
69 b 70 c 71 b 72 b
73 b 74 b 75 b 76 b
77 b 78 a 79 b 80 b
81 a 82 d 83 d 84 a
85 b 86 a 87 c 88 a
89 b 90 c 91 b 92 a
93 c 94 d 95 c 96 d
97 b 98 c 99 d
100 d

HISTORY

1 c   2 a   3 c   4 c
5 d   6 a   7 c   8 d
9 c   10 b 11 a 12 a
13 a 14 c 15 c 16 b
17 d 18 c 19 d 20 b
21 c 22 b 23 d 24 d
25 c 26 b 27 d 28 b
29 a 30 c 31 a 32 b
33 d 34 d 35 d 36 d
37 b 38 a 39 b 40 a
41 c 42 c 43 a 44 a
45 a 46 c 47 b 48 a
49 d 50 c 51 d 52 c
53 d 54 b 55 c 56 c
57 d 58 a 59 a 60 d
61 d 62 a 63 b 64 d
65 c 66 a 67 c 68 a
69 d 70 d 71 b 72 c
73 a 74 d 75 d 76 c
77 c 78 b 79 c 80 a
81 c 82 b 83 c 84 d
85 c 86 b 87 d 88 d
89 c 90 c 91 c 92 d
93 d 94 c 95 a 96 a
97 d 98 a 99 c
100 b 101 a 102 b
103 c 104 c 105 a
106 d 107 c 108 b
109 b 110 a 111 c
112 d 113 a 114 a
115 a 116 a 117 d
118 c 119 c 120 c
121 c 122 c 123 d
124 b 125 c 126 c
127 c 128 a 129 d
130 d 131 b 132 c
133 b 134 b 135 b
136 b 137 d 138 a
139 d 140 a 141 d
142 c 143 a 144 c
145 d 146 c 147 d
148 b 149 d 150 d

GEOGRAPHY

1 d   2 b   3 d   4 a
5 a   6 b   7 c   8 d
9 b   10 c 11 c 12 b
13 c 14 c 15 b 16 c
17 d 18 c 19 c 20 d
21 d 22 d 23 a 24 c
25 a 26 c 27 c 28 b
29 d 30 c 31 b 32 a
33 c 34 d 35 b 36 c
37 b 38 c 39 c 40 c
41 a 42 d 43 d 44 d
45 a 46 a 47 a 48 d
49 d 50 a 51 a 52 a
53 b 54 c 55 b 56 b
57 d 58 d 59 a 60 c
61 b 62 c 63 d 64 a
65 b 66 d 67 a 68 a
69 b 70 c 71 a 72 b
73 c 74 c 75 b 76 d
77 b 78 b 79 c 80 b
81 d 82 c 83 a 84 c
85 d 86 a 87 d 88 c
89 b 90 b 91 d 92 c
93 b 94 d 95 c 96 a
97 c 98 a 99 d
100 a 101 d 102 b
103 c 104 b 105 c
106 a 107 b 108 d
109 d 110 c 111 b
112 c 113 d 114 a
115 d 116 a 117 d
118 d 119 d 120 d
121 b 122 c 123 a
124 c 125 a 126 d
127 b 128 b 129 b
130 d 131 d 132 c
133 a 134 a 135 d
136 d 137 d 138 d
139 a 140 c 141 d
142 a 143 d 144 c
145 b 146 c 147 d
148 a 149 d 150 d

MUSIC

1 c	2 c	3 b	4 b
5 b	6 b	7 a	8 b
9 d	10 d	11 d	12 d
13 b	14 b	15 b	16 b
17 d	18 b	19 c	20 d
21 d	22 c	23 b	24 c
25 a	26 b	27 d	28 b
29 b	30 c	31 b	32 b
33 d	34 c	35 d	36 a
37 a	38 d	39 a	40 d
41 a	42 d	43 c	44 b
45 a	46 b	47 a	48 d
49 d	50 b	51 a	52 c
53 a	54 c	55 c	56 a
57 d	58 b	59 b	60 b
61 a	62 d	63 d	64 a
65 a	66 d	67 d	68 a
69 a	70 d	71 c	72 b
73 d	74 b	75 d	76 a
77 d	78 a	79 d	80 c
81 d	82 c	83 d	84 b
85 c	86 a	87 b	88 b
89 d	90 a		

BUSINESS STUDIES

1 b	2 d	3 c	4 a
5 a	6 d	7 b	8 d
9 c	10 d	11 d	12 d
13 a	14 a	15 d	16 a
17 c	18 a	19 c	20 b
21 b	22 c	23 b	24 d
25 a	26 a	27 d	28 d
29 d	30 b	31 d	32 b
33 b	34 a	35 d	36 b
37 d	38 d	39 b	40 c
41 b	42 c	43 b	44 c
45 a	46 c	47 b	48 a
49 b	50 b	51 d	52 c
53 d	54 c	55 b	56 b

57 b	58 d	59 a	60 b
61 a	62 b	63 c	64 b
65 b	66 b	67 d	68 d
69 c	70 b	71 d	72 d
73 d	74 a	75 a	76 d
77 d	78 c	79 b	80 c
81 b	82 d	83 c	84 a
85 c	86 b	87 a	88 a
89 a	90 d		

RELIGIOUS EDUCATION

1 c	2 a	3 b	4 b
5 b	6 a	7 a	8 d
9 c	10 b	11 b	12 c
13 c	14 b	15 b	16 a
17 c	18 b	19 a	20 b
21 a	22 a	23 c	24 b
25 d	26 a	27 d	28 c
29 b	30 b	31 c	32 b
33 d	34 c	35 c	36 c
37 c	38 c	39 b	40 c
41 b	42 a	43 b	44 a
45 a	46 b	47 c	48 a
49 a	50 d	51 c	52 d
53 b	54 c	55 c	56 a
57 a	58 a	59 b	60 d
61 d	62 c	63 c	64 a
65 c	66 c	67 c	68 c
69 c	70 d	71 a	72 a
73 a	74 d	75 d	76 b
77 a	78 d	79 b	80 b
81 b	82 b	83 d	84 c
85 d	86 d	87 c	88 c
89 b	90 b		